ECONOMIC ISSUES, PROBLEMS AND PERSPECTIVES

GLOBAL COMPETITION

TRADE ADJUSTMENT ASSISTANCE

ECONOMIC ISSUES, PROBLEMS AND PERSPECTIVES

Additional books in this series can be found on Nova's website
under the Series tab.

Additional E-books in this series can be found on Nova's website
under the E-books tab.

TRADE ISSUES, POLICIES AND LAWS

Additional books in this series can be found on Nova's website
under the Series tab.

Additional E-books in this series can be found on Nova's website
under the E-books tab.

ECONOMIC ISSUES, PROBLEMS AND PERSPECTIVES

GLOBAL COMPETITION

TRADE ADJUSTMENT ASSISTANCE

DIANNA J. HALL
AND
KEVIN L. ECHOLLS
EDITORS

Nova Science Publishers, Inc.
New York

For permission to use material from this book please contact us:
Telephone 631-231-7269; Fax 631-231-8175
Web Site: http://www.novapublishers.com

Library of Congress Cataloging-in-Publication Data

Global competition : trade adjustment assistance / editors, Dianna J. Hall and Kevin L. Echolls.
p. cm.
Includes bibliographical references and index.
ISBN 978-1-61324-712-9 (softcover : alk. paper) 1. Trade adjustment assistance--United States. 2. Trade adjustment assistance--Law and legislation--United States. I. Hall, Dianna J. II. Echolls, Kevin L.
HF1421.G57 2011
362.85--dc23

2011016753

Published by Nova Science Publishers, Inc. † New York

CONTENTS

PREFACE

Economists generally acknowledge that trade liberalization enhances the economic welfare of all trade partners, but with stiffer global competition, many firms and workers also face difficult adjustment problems. Congress has responded to these adjustment costs by authorizing four trade adjustment assistance (TAA) programs to assist trade-impacted workers, firms, farmers and communities. This book examines the TAA program, which provides technical assistance to trade-affected firms to help them develop strategies and make other adjustments to remain competitive in the changing international economy.

Chapter 1- Economists generally acknowledge that trade liberalization enhances the economic welfare of all trade partners, but with stiffer global competition, many firms and workers also face difficult adjustment problems. Congress has responded to these adjustment costs by authorizing four trade adjustment assistance (TAA) programs to assist trade-impacted workers, firms, farmers, and communities. This report discusses the TAA program for firms (TAAF). The TAAF program provides technical assistance to trade-affected firms to help them develop strategies and make other adjustments to remain competitive in the changing international economy. The 111th Congress authorized the program through February 12, 2012, and it continues to operate at FY2010 levels of $15.8 million under a continuing resolution.

Chapter 2- The Trade Adjustment Assistance for Farmers (TAAF) program provides technical assistance and cash benefits to producers of agricultural commodities and fishermen who experience adverse economic impacts caused by increased imports. Congress first authorized this program in 2002, and made significant changes to it in the 2009 economic stimulus package (P.L. 111-5). The 2009 revisions were intended to make it easier for commodity producers and fishermen to qualify for program benefits. It also provided over $200 million in funding through year-end 2010. The 2010 omnibus trade measure (P.L. 111-344) temporarily extended the program through February 12, 2011, and authorized an additional $10.4 million.

Chapter 3- Trade Adjustment Assistance for Workers (TAA) provides assistance to qualifying workers who lose their jobs directly due to increased imports or shifts in production out of the United States. Certified workers whose unemployment compensation has ended and who are in approved training may receive income support payments (Trade Readjustment Allowances, or TRA) for a maximum of 156 weeks. Some workers age 50 or older are eligible to receive Reemployment Trade Adjustment Assistance (RTAA), a wage supplement program. Both TAA- and RTAA-eligible workers can receive a Health Coverage Tax Credit (HCTC), which provides a refundable tax credit to offset 80% of the health insurance premiums of TAA- and RTAA-eligible workers. This report provides background on the programs, including a description of the eligibility for these programs and benefits available to participants. It also describes the main changes to the program with the reauthorization and expansion of TAA in the American Recovery and Reinvestment Act of 2009 (ARRA; P.L. 111-5), which was signed into law by President Barack Obama on February 17, 2009. The changes made by ARRA were to expire on December 31, 2010. H.R. 6517, the Omnibus Trade Act of 2010, extended the changes made by ARRA though February 12, 2011. H.R. 6517 passed the House and the Senate on December 22, 2010.

Chapter 4- Trade Adjustment Assistance (TAA) provides income support and training assistance to workers who become unemployed for certain trade-related reasons. Only workers who make an article (i.e., manufacturing workers) are eligible for TAA. Under current law, service workers who become unemployed for a trade-related reason (e.g., outsourcing) are ineligible for TAA. Several bills in the 110th Congress (S. 1848, H.R. 910, H.R. 3589, H.R. 3920) would expand TAA to include service workers and public sector employees. The available data indicates that the number of displaced *manufacturing* workers in offshorable occupations from 2003 to 2005 (489,000) roughly equals the number of TAA-certified manufacturing workers over the same period (450,000). There were 840,000 workers displaced from offshorable *nonmanufacturing* occupations from 2003 to 2005, suggesting that the pool of TAA-eligible workers could have increased by over 170% if service workers had been eligible for TAA. In January 2006, nearly three times as many employed nonmanufacturing workers were in offshorable occupations (20.7 million) than employed manufacturing workers in offshorable occupations (7.7 million), suggesting a large increase in the pool of potentially eligible TAA workers.

Chapter 5- Manufacturing workers face an uncertain future as manufacturing employment declines—more than 3 million manufacturing jobs have been lost in this country since 2000, many due to international trade. Furthermore, finding a new job may be harder for these workers because they tend to be older with have fewer transferable skills than other laid-off workers. The Trade Adjustment Assistance (TAA) program was established in 1962 to assist manufacturing workers who lose their jobs because of international trade. In 2002, the Congress made a number of key changes designed to expand benefits and decrease the time it takes to get workers into services. This testimony draws upon several GAO reports, including our most recently issued TAA report and our case study of five layoffs, and provides an overview of (1) how the TAA program operates, (2) recent trends in the Department of Labor's (Labor) certification of petitions, (3) the extent to which workers participate in training, (4) the extent to which workers take advantage of other TAA benefits, and (5) what is known about TAA program outcomes.

Chapter 6- On August 18, 2009, the Department of Commerce's Economic Development Administration (EDA) published in the *Federal Register* final rules and regulations governing Trade Adjustment Assistance for Communities (TAAC) program. The regulations outline the responsibilities of EDA in administering the program, including determining a community's eligibility for TAAC grants, providing technical assistance to impacted communities, and evaluating grant applications. On January 11, 2010, EDA published in the *Federal Register* a notice soliciting applications for TAAC grants. Concurrently, it published the full announcement and application for assistance at http://www.grants.gov and established April 20, 2010, as the deadline for applications.

In: Global Competition
Editors: Dianna J. Hall et.al
ISBN: 978-1-61324-712-9

Chapter 1

TRADE ADJUSTMENT ASSISTANCE FOR FIRMS: ECONOMIC, PROGRAM, AND POLICY ISSUES

J. F. Hornbeck

SUMMARY

Economists generally acknowledge that trade liberalization enhances the economic welfare of all trade partners, but with stiffer global competition, many firms and workers also face difficult adjustment problems. Congress has responded to these adjustment costs by authorizing four trade adjustment assistance (TAA) programs to assist trade-impacted workers, firms, farmers, and communities. This report discusses the TAA program for firms (TAAF). The TAAF program provides technical assistance to trade-affected firms to help them develop strategies and make other adjustments to remain competitive in the changing international economy. The 111th Congress authorized the program through February 12, 2012, and it continues to operate at FY2010 levels of $15.8 million under a continuing resolution.

Congress first authorized TAA in Title III of the Trade Expansion Act of 1962 (P.L. 87-794), including a new firm and industry assistance program, which is administered by the Economic Development Administration (EDA) of the U.S. Department of Commerce. It provides *technical assistance* to help trade-impacted firms make strategic adjustments, which may allow them to remain competitive in a global economy. Originally firm TAA also included loans and loan guarantees, but Congress eliminated all direct financial assistance in 1986 because of federal budgetary cutbacks and concern over the program's high default rates and limited effectiveness.

Debate early in the 111th Congress over TAA reauthorization led to a February 5, 2009, bipartisan agreement to expand and extend existing programs for workers, firms, and farmers, and to add a fourth program for communities. The agreement became part of the American Recovery and Reinvestment Act of 2009 (P.L. 111-5—the Stimulus Bill). Congress changed the TAA for Firms program in a number of important ways. It expanded eligibility for trade adjustment assistance to include services firms, authorized an extension of the program through December 31, 2010, increased annual authorized funding levels from $16 million to $50 million, provided greater flexibility for a firm to demonstrate eligibility for assistance, established new oversight and evaluation criteria, created a new position of Director of Adjustment Assistance for Firms, and required submission to Congress of a detailed annual report on the TAAF program.

Authorization of the TAA programs was set to expire on January 1, 2011. The Omnibus Trade Act of 2010 (H.R. 6517), which the House and Senate passed on December 22, 2010, extended the TAAF program through February 12, 2012. However, because of expiring language in the act, those expanded provisions covering eligibility for services firms and other matters passed in the ARRA all expired on February 12, 2011, although the program continues to be authorized and operate at FY2010 levels of $15.8 million under the continuing resolution.

On February 8, 2011, S. 308, the Trade Extenders Act of 2011 was introduced in the Senate. This bill would authorize the TAA for Firms program to operate through June 30, 2013. It would also authorize appropriations of $50 million for FY2011 and $37.5 million for the nine months ending June 30, 2012. Because the TAA for Firms program awards grants to the eleven regional Trade Adjustment Assistance Centers (TAACs) on July 1 of the fiscal year, S. 308 would allow grants for FY2011 to be funded at the $50 million level, if Congress fully appropriates that amount, and a nine-month pro rated share ($37.5 million) would be available for FY2012. Funds would be awarded for the grant fiscal year July 1, 2012 through June 30, 2013.

INTRODUCTION

Economists generally acknowledge that trade liberalization enhances the economic welfare of all trade partners, but with stiffer global competition, many firms and workers also face difficult adjustment problems. Congress has responded to these adjustment costs by authorizing four trade adjustment assistance (TAA) programs to assist trade-impacted workers, firms, farmers, and communities. This report discusses the TAA program for firms (TAAF). The TAAF program provides technical assistance to trade-affected firms to help them develop strategies and make other adjustments to remain competitive in the changing international economy. The 111th Congress authorized the program through February 12, 2012, and it continues to operate at FY2010 levels of $15.8 million under a continuing resolution.

RECENT DEVELOPMENTS

Debate early in the 111th Congress over TAA reauthorization led to a February 5, 2009, bipartisan agreement to expand and extend existing programs for workers, firms, and farmers, and to add a fourth program for communities. The agreement became part of the American Recovery and Reinvestment Act (ARRA) of 2009 (P.L. 111-5—the Stimulus Bill). Congress changed the TAA for Firms program in a number of important ways. It expanded eligibility for trade adjustment assistance to include services firms, authorized an extension of the program through December 31, 2010, increased annual funding levels from $16 million to $50 million, provided greater flexibility for a firm to demonstrate eligibility for assistance, established new oversight and evaluation criteria, created a new position of Director of Adjustment Assistance for Firms, and required submission to Congress of a detailed annual report on the TAAF program.

Authorization of the TAA programs was set to expire on January 1, 2011. The Omnibus Trade Act of 2010 (H.R. 6517), which the House and Senate passed on December 22, 2010, extended the TAAF program through February 12, 2012.[1] However, because of expiring language in the act, those expanded provisions covering eligibility for services firms and other matters passed in the ARRA all expired on February 12, 2011, although the program remains authorized and continues to operate at FY2010 levels of $15.8 million under a continuing resolution.

On February 8, 2011, S. 308, the Trade Extenders Act of 2011 was introduced in the Senate. This bill would authorize the TAAF program to operate through June 30, 2013. It would also authorize appropriations of $50 million for FY20 11 and $37.5 million for the nine months of FY2012 ending June 30, 2012.

The TAAF program operates by awarding grants to the regional Trade Adjustment Assistance Centers (TAACs). The grants are awarded on July 1 of the fiscal year in which appropriations are made. Therefore, TAACs are currently working off FY2010 funds and the TAACs are scheduled to be awarded FY2011 grants on July 1, 2011, so no interruption of operations in the near term is expected. However, the program is funded under a continuing resolution. The implications of S. 308 are, that if passed by Congress, grants for FY2011 would be funded at the $50 million level, with a nine-month pro rated portion ($37.5 million) made available for FY2012. Grants would likely be awarded to TAACs on July 1 of that year.

THE ECONOMICS OF TRADE ADJUSTMENT

Economists tend to agree that in defining the rules of exchange among countries, freer trade is preferable to protectionism. Insights from traditional trade theory (comparative advantage) point to the mutual gains for countries trading on their differences, producing those goods at which they are relatively more efficient, while trading for those at which they are relatively less so. Additional gains are realized from similar, intra-industry trade based on efficiencies from segmented and specialized production.[2] Firm-level evidence supports theory. Trade appears to "enable efficient producers within an industry, and efficient industries within an economy, to expand," leading to a reallocation of resources that increases a country's productivity, output, and income.[3] Consumers (both firms and households) also gain from a wider variety of goods at lower prices.

It is also true, and commonly cited, that increased competition from trade liberalization creates both "winners and losers," presenting adjustment problems for all countries. The more efficient firms and plants may grow as they expand into overseas markets; the less efficient may contract, merge, or perhaps even fail when faced with greater foreign competition. While the adjustment process may be healthy from a macroeconomic perspective, much like market-driven adjustments that occur for reasons other than trade (e.g., technological change), it can be a harsh transition for some firms and their workers.[4]

Critics of free trade agreements often highlight the adjustment costs of reducing trade barriers. To avoid business closures and layoffs, trade-impacted firms often seek to weaken, if not defeat, trade liberalizing legislation. This makes economic sense from the perspective of affected industries, firms, and workers, but economists argue that in the long run it can be more costly for the country as a whole. The costs of protection arise because competition is suppressed, reducing pressure on firms to innovate, operate more efficiently, and become lower cost producers. The brunt of these costs falls to consumers, both individuals and businesses, who must pay higher prices, but the national economy is also denied higher standards of living because of forgone productivity gains.

One way to balance the large and broad-based gains from freer trade with the smaller and more highly concentrated costs is to address the needs of firms negatively affected. Congress has done so in authorizing the trade adjustment assistance (TAA) programs, including the one for firms.[5]

Supporters justify TAA policy on grounds that (1) it helps those who are hurt by trade liberalization (the "losers"), (2) the economic costs are lower than protectionism and can be borne by society as a whole ("the winners"), and (3) given rigidities in the adjustment process, it helps redeploy economic resources more quickly, thereby reducing productivity losses and related public sector costs (e.g., unemployment compensation).

The Firm Trade Adjustment Assistance Program[6]

Congress first authorized TAA in Title III of the Trade Expansion Act of 1962 (P.L. 87-794), including a new firm and industry assistance program, which is administered by the Economic Development Administration (EDA) of the U.S. Department of Commerce.[7] It provides *technical assistance* to help trade-impacted firms make strategic adjustments that may allow them to remain competitive in a global economy. Originally, firm TAA also included loans and loan guarantees, but Congress eliminated all direct financial assistance in 1986 because of federal budgetary cutbacks and concern over the program's high default rates and limited effectiveness. Congress has amended the program many times over the nearly half century it has been in existence, most recently in the American Recovery and Reinvestment Act of 2009 (P.L. 111-5). Key changes include extending eligibility to services firms, increasing funding, and introducing greater flexibility to demonstrate eligibility for assistance.

TAA authorizations and appropriations for fiscal years 2000-2010 appear in **Table 1**. The TAA for firms program has been reauthorized through December 31, 2010, at an annual level of $50 million. Historically, appropriated funds have fallen short of authorized spending levels, which remains the case under the most recent authorization and appropriations acts.

In practice, technical assistance is provided through one of the 11 Trade Adjustment Assistance Centers (TAACs), which apply for grants from EDA to operate their programs. All appropriated funds have been used to support the TAAC process; no funds go directly to firms. TAACs may operate through universities, private firms, or non-profit associations. They provide or contract for technical assistance to assist firms from the initial certification process through implementation of the adjustment proposal. TAACs are staffed by professionals with broad business expertise who can help firms develop "recovery strategies" and also identify financial resources. They are, in effect, consultants specializing in business turnaround strategies specific to the needs of each firm, which typically faces adjustments in many areas to compete with lower- priced imports.[8]

Eligibility and Certification

The process for receiving TAA unfolds in three phases. First, a firm must submit a petition to become certified as eligible. EDA is statutorily required to accept or reject the petition within 40 days of receiving all materials. The firm must demonstrate eligibility by documenting that (1) "a significant number or proportion of workers"[9] in the firm have become or are threatened to become totally or partially separated; (2) sales, production, or both of a firm "decreased absolutely;"[10] and (3) increased imports of competing articles "contributed importantly"[11] to the decline in sales, production, and/or workforce. Declines in these variables must be demonstrated, but may be done so in five different ways to establish "minimum certification thresholds" for eligibility:

- **Twelve-month decline**—using all three criteria, compare the most recent 12-month period for which data are available with the immediately preceding 12-month period.

- **Twelve-month versus twenty-four-month decline**—using all three criteria, compare the most recent 12-month period for which data are available with the immediately preceding 24-month period, using average annual data for sales and production.
- **Twelve-month versus thirty-six-month decline**—using all three criteria, compare the most recent 12-month period for which data are available with the immediately preceding 36-month period, using average annual data for sales and production.
- **Interim sales or production decline**—using all three criteria, but defining a base period based on sales and production figures that compares at a minimum a most recent six-month period during the most recent 12-month period for which data are available, with data in the same six-month period for the immediately preceding 12-month period.
- **Interim employment decline**— using all three criteria, but defining a base period based on employment data that compares at a minimum a most recent six- month period during the most recent 12-month period for which data are available with data in the same six-month period for the immediately preceding 12-month period.

Second, once certified as eligible, a firm has two years to develop and submit its adjustment proposal. Approval of the adjustment proposal depends on EDA's finding that it (1) is reasonably calculated "to materially contribute" to the economic adjustment of the firm; (2) gives adequate consideration to the interests of the firm's workers; and (3) demonstrates that the firm will use its own resources for adjustment. EDA typically makes a determination within two to four weeks. Third, the firm has five years to implement an approved adjustment proposal. The standard time to completion tends to be within two years.[12]

Table 1. Firm TAA Authorizations and Appropriations, FY2000-2010 ($ millions).

	2000	2001	2002	2003	2004	2005	2006	2007	2008	2009	2010
Authorizations	10.0	10.0	10.0	16.0	16.0	16.0	16.0	16.0	16.0	50.0	50.0
Appropriations	10.5	10.5	10.5	10.0	11.9	11.0	12.8	12.8	14.1	15.8	15.8

Data Source: U.S. Department of Commerce. Economic Development Administration and P.L. 111-5.

EDA can provide technical assistance to a firm for preparation of the petition for eligibility certification, and to a certified eligible firm for developing and implementing an approved adjustment proposal. There is no cost for assistance provided in developing the petition, but the firm must pay at least 25% of the cost to prepare the adjustment proposal and at least 25% of any awarded adjustment assistance. For project assistance exceeding $30,000, a firm must cover at least 50% of the total cost.[13] In practice, because technical assistance is provided in the preparation of the petition, there is a high formal acceptance rate likely because petitions are completed correctly and poor proposals or candidates can be weeded out early in the process.

The TAACs also provide detailed assistance in formulation of the adjustment proposal, which seeks to identify business planning and practices that can be enhanced to improve firm competitiveness in at least three major areas. First, since firms must be experiencing falling sales or declining production to be eligible, TAACs often focus on marketing or sales strategies to identify new markets, new products, promotional initiatives, and export opportunities. Second, production inefficiencies are corrected to reduce firm costs and improve price competitiveness. Third, TAACs can develop debt restructuring strategies and frequently act as intermediaries in finding new sources of business financing. In 2009, 65% of petitioning firms proposed projects to improve marketing-sales or production-engineering, and 35% proposed projects to enhance support services or management systems. [14]

Table 2. summarizes trade adjustment data for fiscal years 2003-2009. The TAAF program targets small- and medium-sized enterprises (SMEs), which is borne out in the firm data. In 2009, firms tended to have fewer than 100 employees and less than $11 million in sales. The federal government provided 48.5% of adjustment costs, for an average $60,123 per firm.

Program Evaluation

Historically, program evaluation has been limited, lacking a formal evaluation process. Congress addressed this issue by requiring EDA to submit an annual report on the TAAF program by December 15 of each year. Earlier efforts to analyze the TAAF program include comprehensive studies by the Urban Institute in 1998 and the Government Accountability Office (GAO) in 2000.[15]

Table 2. Trade Adjustment Assistance, Select Program Indicators for FY2003-2009.

	2003	2004	2005	2006	2007	2008	2009
Number of Firms Assisted	162	177	132	137	126	139	172
Avg Firm Sales (millions)	$7.2	$11.6	$8.4	$10.6	$11.2	$13.1	10.7
Avg Firm Employees	68	88	64	91	68	82	77
Govt Share (millions)	$8.1	$8.5	$5.9	$6.7	$7.1	$7.9	10.3
Firm Share (millions)	$7.4	$8.1	$5.4	$6.0	$5.9	$7.5	9.8
Total TAA (millions)	$15.5	$16.6	$11.3	$12.7	$13.0	$15.4	20.2
Avg TAA Per Firm[a]	$50,000	$48,023	$44,697	$48,905	$56,449	$56,827	60,123

Data Source: U.S. Department of Commerce. Economic Development Administration.

[a] Government share of TAA Firm program divided by the number of accepted adjustment proposals.

Both found deficiencies with the TAAF program, such as a cumbersome certification process, long approval times, and little oversight and evaluation of projects. Many of these criticisms have been corrected. The petition and adjustment proposal approval process has been automated and streamlined. In fact, over the past two years, the time between submission of petitions for certification and acceptance has fallen from an average of 28 to 11 days. The average time between acceptance of the petition and certification has been 45 days, higher than the statutory 40 days. EDA notes that a 49% increase in petitions caused processing time to increase for 2009.[16]

EDA reports that TAACs are now allocated funds in part based on performance measures (number of firm certifications and adjustment proposals generated) and quality measures developed in part from a firm survey feedback mechanism. Created by Dunn & Bradstreet, it is intended to provide some indication of "successful interventions" and "program best practices." This survey has helped reduce the time between submission of the petition and approval of final adjustment proposal.[17] Anecdotal evidence points to numerous "success" stories, but more sophisticated analysis is needed to estimate the effectiveness of this program approach. It is difficult to isolate the effects of the firm TAA program in determining why a particular firm might succeed in its turnaround effort. Previous studies mentioned above have suggested that many firms might have been able to do so on their own. The fact that small- and medium-sized firms are targeted, however, suggests that the program is attempting to reach that pool of firms most vulnerable to increased globalization and with the fewest resources for undertaking adjustment. Without a more in-depth analysis, however, the issue of TAAF effectiveness remains a somewhat speculative, if not open question.

Economic and Policy Issues

By any measure, firm and industry trade adjustment assistance is a small federal program; it remains, nonetheless, controversial. Critics point to fundamental arguments opposing TAA that have been debated since before the program was initiated in 1962. First, if competition resulting from trade liberalization is not considered "unfair trade," why should the federal government be involved? Second, why should federal assistance be necessary for adjustment to trade competition when there is no similar assistance for adjustment to domestic competitive pressures? Third, should not this adjustment process simply be accepted as part of a dynamic market economy working to allocate resources more efficiently and in a way that is in the country's long-term interests?

Proponents of the program argue that TAA is only modestly funded and provides benefits to firms, owners, managers, and workers that amount to many times the value of federal expenditures. Also, if changes in national trade policy have altered the rules under which businesses compete, does not the federal government have some responsibility for assisting firms that bear the costs of adjustment?[18] Finally, a point in favor of firm TAA is that it focuses on adjustment, not long-term financial assistance. Firms must commit their own resources and have every incentive to adjust successfully to ensure their very survival. They are not faced with the potential for dependency on long-term cash payments, which critics charge is a problem with some federal assistance programs.

In addition to economic concerns, political considerations also define the TAA debate. Congress has accepted, with some reservations, that freer trade is in the long-term interests of the United States. While those skeptical of trade liberalization may support TAA for the assistance it provides to affected workers and firms, proponents of freer trade may also embrace TAA as a complement to an open trade policy along with other domestic economic policy adjustments.[19] To the extent that TAA can address some of the concerns of adversely affected firms, it may support trade liberalization as a continuing foundation of U.S. trade policy and temper calls for relief through increased tariffs, quotas, or other restrictions on trade. Advocates of trade liberalization may find support for firm TAA as compelling from a cost-benefit perspective, if it leads to broader acceptance of trade opening legislation.

End Notes

[1] This legislation affected the workers program more, with many provisions expired on February 12, 2011. See: CRS Report RL34383, *Trade Adjustment Assistance (TAA) for Workers: Current Issues and Legislation*, by John J. Topoleski.

[2] For an accessible summary of these effects, see Paul Krugman, "The Increasing Returns Revolution in Trade and Geography," *American Economic Review*, vol. 99, no. 3 (June 2009), pp. 561-571.

[3] On how trade affects total factor productivity based on U.S. manufacturing firm and plant level data, see Bernard, Andrew B. and J. Bradford Jensen, "Exporting and Productivity in the USA," *Oxford Review of Economic Policy*, vol. 20, no. 3 (2004). pp. 343-344, 350, 352, and 356.

[4] Both the benefits and costs of trade derive from resources moving from less to more productive plants (intra-industry) and firms (inter-industry). Employment dislocation is the most

noticeable cost, giving rise to congressional interest in TAA programs. Ibid., pp. 345 and 356.

[5] Howard F. Rosen, *Strengthening Trade Adjustment Assistance*, Peterson Institute for International Economics, Policy Brief PB08-2, Washington, D.C., January 2008, pp. 1-2.

[6] Based on 13 C.F.R. § 315, which provides details for applying for TAAF assistance. Note that many of these rules expired on February 12, 2011 and it remains to be seen if Congress will reinstate them.

[7] The TAA for firms program was originally administered jointly by the Tariff Commission (predecessor to the USITC) and the U.S. Department of Commerce.

[8] P.L. 93-618, Section 253, as amended and U.S. Department of Commerce. Economic Development Administration. http://www.taacenters.org.

[9] 5% of a firm's work force or 50 workers, whichever is less, with EDA discretion to set other parameters in special cases.

[10] A firm's sales or production or both (or of any article or service that accounted for not less than 25% of total sales or production) have declined by a minimum of 5% relative to statutory comparison guidelines below.

[11] A cause which is important, but not necessarily more important than any other cause. A firm must provide a list of four important customers, of which the TAAC must interview two, to help evaluate whether the firm has been "trade- impacted." U.S. Department of Commerce. Economic Development Administration, "Program Announcement for the Trade Adjustment Assistance for Firms Program," 73 *Federal Register* 6925, February 6, 2008.

[12] U.S. Department of Commerce. Economic Development Administration, "Trade Adjustment Assistance for Firms Program Fiscal Year 2009 Annual Report," 75 *Federal Register*, January 15, 2010, p. 2495.

[13] 13 CFR 315.6 (c)(2) and Federal Register. *Program Announcement for the Trade Adjustment Assistance for Firms Program*. February 6, 2008. Vol. 73. No. 25. p. 6925

[14] U.S. Department of Commerce. Economic Development Administration, "Trade Adjustment Assistance for Firms Program Fiscal Year 2009 Annual Report," 75 *Federal Register* 2492, January 15, 2010, p. 2508.

[15] U.S. Department of Commerce. Economic Development Administration. *Effective Aid to Trade-Impacted Manufacturers: An Evaluation of the Trade Adjustment Assistance Program*. Prepared by the Urban Institute, Washington, D.C., November 1998 and. GAO. *Trade Adjustment Assistance: Impact of Federal Assistance to Firms Is Unclear*. Report GAO-01-12. Washington, DC. December 2000.

[16] U.S. Department of Commerce. Economic Development Administration, "Trade Adjustment Assistance for Firms Program Fiscal Year 2009 Annual Report," 75 *Federal Register* 249 1-2495, January 15, 2010.

[17] U.S. Department of Commerce. Economic Development Administration, "Program Announcement for the Trade Adjustment Assistance for Firms Program," 73 *Federal Register* 6926, February 6, 2008 and correspondence with EDA.

[18] Citing President Kennedy prior to congressional passage of the first TAA statute, "There is an obligation to render assistance to those who suffer as a result of national trade policy." Howard F. Rosen, *Strengthening Trade Adjustment Assistance*, Peterson Institute for International Economics, Policy Brief PB08-2, Washington, D.C., January 2008, p. 1.

[19] Ibid.

In: Global Competition
Editors: Dianna J. Hall et al.
ISBN: 978-1-61324-712-9

Chapter 2

TRADE ADJUSTMENT ASSISTANCE FOR FARMERS

Remy Jurenas

SUMMARY

The Trade Adjustment Assistance for Farmers (TAAF) program provides technical assistance and cash benefits to producers of agricultural commodities and fishermen who experience adverse economic impacts caused by increased imports. Congress first authorized this program in 2002, and made significant changes to it in the 2009 economic stimulus package (P.L. 111-5). The 2009 revisions were intended to make it easier for commodity producers and fishermen to qualify for program benefits. It also provided over $200 million in funding through year-end 2010. The 2010 omnibus trade measure (P.L. 111-344) temporarily extended the program through February 12, 2011, and authorized an additional $10.4 million.

The U.S. Department of Agriculture (USDA) is required to follow a two-step process in administering TAAF program benefits. First, a group of producers must be certified eligible to apply. Second, a producer in a certified group must meet specified requirements to be approved to receive technical assistance and cash payments.

To be certified, a group must show that imports were a significant cause for at least a 15% decline in one of the following factors: the price of the commodity, the quantity of the commodity produced, or the production value of the commodity.

Once a producer group is certified, an individual producer within that group must meet three requirements to be approved for program benefits. These include technical assistance with a training component, and financial assistance. A producer must show that (1) the commodity was produced in the current and also in one recent previous year, (2) the quantity of the commodity produced decreased compared to that in a previous year, or the price received for the commodity decreased compared to a preceding three-year average price, and (3) no benefits were received under any other trade adjustment assistance program. The training component is intended to help the producer become more competitive in producing the same or another commodity. Financial assistance (capped at $12,000 over a three-year period) is to be used by the producer to develop and implement a business adjustment plan designed to address the impact of import competition.

Since 2009, USDA has certified 11 of the 30 petitions filed by various commodity groups and fishermen (e.g., producers of shrimp, catfish, asparagus, lobster, and blueberries). USDA already has approved about 4,500 agricultural producers for training and cash assistance under the three FY2010 certifications. USDA in early 2011 will approve producers under the eight FY2011 certified petitions. Most of the program benefits in both years are expected to flow to shrimp producers.

Because TAAF funding expired on February 12, 2011, the 112th Congress is considering proposals to provide future funding. S. 308 would extend TAAF and the other TAA programs (among other provisions) through mid-2012. An effort in the House to temporarily extend TAA authorities through June 30, 2011, become caught up in criticism of their rationale and linked to the consideration of other trade issues. Some Members want to tie a TAA extension to (1) the Obama Administration making a commitment on a timetable to submit pending free trade agreements with Colombia and Panama to Congress for a vote and (2) the terms of extending one trade preference program.

Rationale for Program

The origin of the Trade Adjustment Assistance for Farmers program can be traced back to a 2000 Department of Labor report recommending that a separate program be enacted "to assist agricultural producers and workers affected adversely by imports" if the objective is to assist them to remain in their current occupations. The report described the existing trade adjustment assistance (TAA) programs that provided (1) limited technical assistance to help business firms (including some that produced agricultural and food products) regain economic competitiveness or to shift into producing other goods, and (2) training assistance to workers (including those employed by some agricultural firms) to facilitate their transition into other occupations. It noted that the provision of direct financial assistance (such as income supplements) to farmers, or efforts to financially enable them to continue producing the commodity adversely affected by imports rather than help them adjust to employment in other sectors, would be inconsistent with the objectives of the then-existing TAA programs.[1]

Observers stated that farmers and ranchers typically did not qualify for the TAA workers program because they were self-employed (and thus rarely were eligible for unemployment benefits) and were less likely to want to be retrained for a new occupation (particularly if earning income from producing other crops or from non-farm sources). Others pointed out that agricultural producers most likely to be affected by import surges produce a commodity that receives little or no price protection nor direct payments under traditional farm subsidy programs. Frequently cited is the impact of increased competition that U.S. fruit and vegetable growers, as well as livestock producers, have encountered due to imports from Mexico and Canada under the North American Free Trade Agreement.[2]

Overview of TAAF Program

The Trade Act of 2002 established a new Trade Adjustment Assistance for Farmers (TAAF) program.[3] It is administered by the U.S. Department of Agriculture's (USDA) Foreign Agricultural Service (FAS). As amended by the enacted 2009 economic stimulus package (P.L. 111-5, Division B, Subtitle I),[4] the program assists agricultural producers who have been adversely affected by competition from imports of a commodity that they produce. An "agricultural commodity producer" is defined as a "person that shares in the risk of producing an agricultural commodity and that is entitled to a share of the commodity for marketing, including an operator, a sharecropper, or a person that owns or rents the land on which the commodity is produced," or a person who reports a gain or loss on a federal income tax return from "the trade or business of fishing." Support is available in the form of enhanced technical assistance and seed money to enable a producer to formulate and implement a business adjustment plan. Producers of raw and natural agricultural commodities (crops, livestock, farm-raised aquatic products, and wild-caught seafood that competes with aquaculture products) and of "any class of goods within an agricultural commodity" must follow a two-part process to receive benefits.

First, a producer group must be certified by USDA as eligible to apply for program benefits (see "Requirements for a Commodity Group to be Certified"). Second, if the group is certified, individual producers in that group must meet certain requirements to be approved to receive technical assistance and cash payments (see "Individual Producer Eligibility Requirements" and "Program Benefits").

Requirements for a Commodity Group to be Certified

A group of agricultural producers can petition the Secretary of Agriculture to be certified as eligible to participate in the TAAF program (i.e., to qualify for benefits). To certify a commodity group, the Secretary must determine that the increase in imports of the agricultural commodity produced by members of the group "contributed importantly"[5] to at least a 15% decline in the national average price, quantity of production, or value of production or cash receipts of the commodity. In making a determination, the Secretary must compare the volume of imports of "articles like or directly competitive with the agricultural commodity" produced by the group in the marketing year in which the petition is filed, to the average volume of imports in the three preceding marketing years. The addition of two other qualifying factors—"quantity of production" and "value of production/cash receipts"—besides price gives the Secretary greater flexibility in determining if a commodity group is eligible to access program benefits.[6] The Secretary has 40 days to make a determination on a group's petition.

Individual Producer Eligibility Requirements

If the Secretary certifies that a group qualifies for assistance, each producer in the group has 90 days to apply for TAAF benefits. To be eligible, an individual producer must show in the application submitted to USDA that (1) the agricultural commodity was produced in the year covered by the group's petition and in at least one of the three preceding marketing years, (2) the quantity of the commodity produced in that year has decreased compared to the amount produced in a previous year, or the price received for the commodity in that year has decreased compared to the average price received in the preceding three marketing years,[7] and (3) no cash benefits were received under the TAA for Workers and TAA for Firms programs, nor were benefits received based on producing another commodity eligible for TAAF assistance.[8]

Program Benefits

The changes enacted in 2009 refocus the TAAF program by (1) making technical assistance available to an eligible producer, and (2) providing financial resources so that a producer can put into effect a business plan to make adjustments in the operation.

A producer approved for the TAAF program is entitled to receive initial technical assistance (TA) to improve competitiveness in the production and marketing of the commodity certified to receive benefits. Such assistance is to include information on what steps could be taken to improve the yield and marketing of that commodity, and on exploring the feasibility and desirability of substituting one or more alternative commodities for the one being produced. USDA can provide supplemental assistance to cover reasonable transportation and subsistence expenses that a producer incurs in accessing initial technical assistance if provided in a location outside a normal commuting distance.

A producer who completes this initial phase is eligible to participate in intensive technical assistance. These include training courses to assist the producer in improving the competitiveness of the same commodity or an alternative commodity, and financial assistance to develop an initial business plan based on the courses completed. USDA is required to approve a producer's initial business plan if it reflects the skills gained by the producer through the courses taken. Further, this plan must demonstrate how the producer will apply these skills to his circumstances. If the plan is approved, the producer is entitled to not more than $4,000 to implement this plan, or to develop a long-term business adjustment plan.

A producer who completes the intensive phase and whose initial business plan has been approved is then eligible for assistance to develop a long-term business adjustment plan. USDA is required to approve this adjustment plan if it includes steps calculated to materially contribute to the producer's economic adjustment to changing market conditions, takes into account the interests of the workers employed by the producer, and demonstrates that the producer will have sufficient resources to implement the business plan. If approved, the producer is entitled to $8,000 to implement this long-term plan.[9]

Limitations on Producer Financial Assistance

The amount of assistance that a producer can receive to implement both the initial business plan and the long-term business adjustment plan is limited to $12,000 in the 36-month period after USDA has certified producers of the commodity as eligible for TAAF benefits.[10] Further, TAAFeligible producers cannot receive cash benefits under any other TAA program.

An applicant is ineligible for TAAF assistance in any year in which his average adjusted gross income exceeds the level specified in Section 1001D of the Food Security Act of 1985 as amended (i.e., $500,000 of non-farm income, or $750,000 of farm income, depending on the details of the applicant's involvement in a farm operation, beginning with the 2009 crop year).[11]

Written Notices to Producers

The Secretary of Agriculture is required to provide written notice to each agricultural commodity producer in a group certified as eligible to receive benefits. A notice stating the benefits available to certified producers must also be published in newspapers of general circulation in the areas in which such producers reside.

Program Coordination

When notified by the International Trade Commission (ITC) that it has begun a safeguard investigation of a particular agricultural commodity, the Secretary of Agriculture is required to conduct a study of (1) the number of agricultural commodity producers who are producing a competitive commodity who have been or are likely to be certified eligible for TAAF, and (2) the extent to which existing programs could facilitate producers' adjustment to import competition.[12] A safeguard (e.g., in the form of additional tariffs, expanded quota, or another restriction on imports) is intended to provide relief from the adverse impact of imports when temporary protection will enable the domestic sector (i.e., producers) to make adjustments to meet import competition.

Within 15 days after the ITC has determined whether or not injury has occurred and reported its recommendations to the President, the Secretary must submit a report to the President on the USDA study's findings.

Program Funding

Section 1887 of P.L. 111-5 authorized and appropriated $90 million in each of FY2009 and FY2010, and $22.5 million for the first quarter of FY2011 (i.e., October to December 2010).[13] This provision also specified that funding shall cover the costs of administering the TAAF program, as well as the salaries and expenses of USDA employees who administer it. Conferees dropped a Senate provision (Section 170 1(c)) that would have made TAAF funding available retroactively (i.e., back to January 1, 2008). In separate congressional action taken to temporarily extend the program, P.L. 111-344 authorizes $10.4 million for the January 1 to February 12, 2011, period.[14] If available funds are not sufficient to meet the commitments for adjustment assistance for eligible producers in any year, the amounts paid out are required to be reduced proportionately.

Expiration of TAAF Program Benefits

With the six-week extension of TAAF funding , producers will be able to access technical and financial assistance through February 12, 2012, if their eligibility had been established, they had applied for program benefits, and USDA had approved their application, by February 12, 2011. Program benefits also will be available to any group of producers that files a petition for certification before February 13, 2011, if USDA determines that the group is eligible. In both cases, benefits will be available to the extent that funds are available and only to those approved to receive technical and financial assistance.[15]

TAAF Program Implementation

Because Congress in 2009 significantly revised TAAF's statutory provisions from those initially enacted, the following describes how this program operated in the period before, and then in the period, after these changes. The break between periods reflects the lack of program authority in the January to September 2008 period.

FY2003-December 2007

Activity under the TAAF in the FY2003-December 2007 period was much lower than authorized funding levels because of low producer participation and low payments, according to the Government Accountability Office (GAO).[16] Of the $459 million authorized for the 5¼-year period through December 31, 2007, budget outlays totaled almost $48 million, according to USDA's Office of Inspector General (OIG) and USDA's Foreign Agricultural Service.[17] This included $27.7 million in cash benefits paid to producers, $9.5 million for technical assistance, and $10.5 million for administrative costs (**Table 1**).

Of the 72 petitions filed by producer groups for assistance during the five-year period that USDA received petitions, USDA certified or approved 30 groups. Shrimp and salmon producers accounted for most of the cash benefits paid out. Producers of Concord grapes, lychees, olives, wild blueberries, fresh potatoes, Florida avocadoes, snapdragons, and catfish were among others that USDA certified to be eligible for assistance. About 8,400 producers qualified for cash payments (**Table 2**).

FY2009 to Present

Administrative Actions

On August 25, 2009, USDA's Foreign Agricultural Service published a proposed rule to establish procedures for a group to request certification of eligibility, and for individual producers to apply for technical assistance and cash benefits, under the amended TAAF program.[18]

On March 1, 2010, USDA issued the TAAF interim rule and announced it will immediately begin to implement the FY2010 program. This allowed producer groups to submit petitions to be certified for eligibility, which if approved, permit individual members of a group to apply for program benefits.[19] For the FY2010 round, USDA accepted petitions through April 14, 2010. If a petition was approved, eligible producers had to file applications for assistance within 90 days of the certification.

Table 1. TAAF Funding, and Outlays by Type, FY2003-FY2011 ($ in millions).

Outlays					
Fiscal Year	**Funding Authority**	**Cash Payments to Producers**	**Technical Assistance Training**	**Administrative Costs**	**Total**
FY2003	90	0.0	3.6	2.6	6.2
FY2004	90	12.6	0.8	2.9	16.3
FY2005	90	14.4	4.1	2.4	20.9
FY2006	90	0.7	1.0	1.6	3.3
FY2007	90	—	—	1.0	—
FY2008[a]	9				
Subtotal, FY2003- FY2008	**459**	**27.7**	**9.5**	**10.5**	**47.7**
FY2009	90	0.0	19.6	5.4	25.0
FY2010	90	71.8	16.4	1.7	90.0
FY2011	32.9[b]	22.5			22.5
Subtotal, FY2009-FY2011	**212.9**	**94.3**	**36.0[c]**	**7.1**	**137.5**
TOTAL, FY2003-FY2011	**671.9**	**122.0**	**45.5**	**17.6[d]**	**185.2**

Source: P.L. 107-210, P.L. 110-89, P.L. 111-5, H.R. 6517, section 101 (c)(12), for funding authority; USDA, OIG (for FY2003 – FY2006 outlays); USDA, Foreign Agricultural Service (for FY2007, FY2009 – FY2011 outlays).

a. Funding was authorized only through December 31, 2007, However, USDA did not implement the TAAF program during this three-month period of FY2008.

b. P.L. 111-344 added an additional $10.4 million to the $22.5 million earlier authorized by P.L. 111-5 for October-December 2010.

c. Under contract with the University of Minnesota.

d. Reflecting implementation by four USDA agencies: Foreign Agricultural Service, Economic Research Service, Farm Service Agency, and National Institute of Food and Agriculture (formerly named Cooperative, State Research, Education, and Extension Service).

Table 2. Activity Under Trade Adjustment Assistance for Farmers Program, FY2003-FY20011.

Fiscal Year	Certification Process		Producer Applicants Covered by Certified Petitions
	Petitions Filed	Petitions Certified	
FY2003	0	—	—
FY2004	25	12	4,512
FY2005	20	14	3,686
FY2006	19	4	208
FY2007	8	0	—
FY2008[a]	—	—	—
Subtotal, FY2003-FY2008	**72**	**30**	**8,406**
FY2009	0	—	—
FY2010	11	3	4,500[b]
FY2011	19	8	[c]
Subtotal, FY2009-FY2011	**30**	**11**	**4,500[d]**
TOTAL, FY2003-FY2011	**102**	**41**	**12,906[d]**

Source: U.S. International Trade Commission, 2004 to 2008 issues of *The Year in Trade;* USDA, FAS, press releases and email communication for FY2009-2011 activity.

a. Program not active because authority expired on December 31, 2007.

b. Estimate

c. Data will be available in early 2011.

d. Incomplete, because FY2011 data is not yet available.

On May 21, 2010, USDA announced that it will accept petitions for the FY2011 TAAF program through July 16, 2010. USDA in late September certified three of the 11 groups that had submitted petitions. Eligible producers had until late December 2010 to file applications for assistance.

Certifications and Producer Approvals

With the 2009 changes to the TAAF program that eased the criteria for a producer group to be certified and for individual producers to be approved for program assistance, more of the provided funding has been used than in the FY2003-December 2007 period. USDA has committed nearly $138 million of the $213 million authorized for the almost 21/2-year period through mid-February 2011. This includes $94.3 million in cash benefits and training costs for producers, $36.0 million for developing the technical assistance resources to be used to provide training , and $7.1 million for administrative costs (**Table 1**). Program outlays committed through December 2010 represent 65% of the authorized funding. (For comparison, outlays in the earlier FY2003-December 2007 period accounted for just over 10% of funding authority.)

Of the 30 petitions filed since FY2009 by producer groups seeking certification (i.e., eligibility to qualify for assistance), USDA certified 11 groups. These included producers of shrimp, catfish, lobsters, asparagus, and wild blueberries. USDA subsequently approved about 4,500 producers for training assistance and cash benefits in FY2010 (**Table 2**). The number that qualify under the FY2011 program (against a late December 2010 deadline) will become known in early 2011. USDA expects that most of the benefits during these two years will flow to shrimp producers in Alaska and along the Gulf and southern Atlantic states. With the program's extension only for six weeks, USDA may not have enough time to accept additional petitions from producer groups. Instead, the $10.4 million authorized through mid-February 2011 may be tapped to meet outstanding commitments to already approved FY2011 applicants.

LEGISLATIVE OUTLOOK IN THE 112TH CONGRESS

Because TAAF funding expired on February 12, 2011, Congress continues to consider proposals to extend program and funding authority. S. 308 (the Trade Extenders Act of 2011) would extend all TAA programs through June 30, 2012. Funding for the TAAF program would be authorized at $90 million for FY2011, and $67.5 million for nine months in FY2012. This bill also would (1) amend health insurance coverage for certain TAA recipients, and (2) extend two trade preference programs that provide duty-free treatment for eligible imported products through mid- 2012—the Generalized System of Preferences[20] and the Andean Trade Preference (ATPA)[21] program.

The House had planned on February 8, 2011, to consider an unnumbered bill under suspension of the rules to extend all TAA programs through June 30, 2011, and to extend the ATPA program. For this 41/2-month period, the TAAF program would be funded at $34 million. Opposition over the budget offset proposed to cover TAA programs' costs, and criticism of the rationale for all TAA programs, led House leadership to pull this measure from the floor schedule. Some Republican Members of the House have suggested that floor consideration of this bill be linked to the Obama Administration committing to a timetable to submit the Colombia and Panama free trade agreements to

Congress for consideration. Some House Democratic members have countered they will not support extending the ATPA trade preference program that benefits Colombia and Ecuador unless the House bill also extends TAA program authority. [22]

End Notes

[1] Department of Labor, "Report on Trade Adjustment Assistance for Agricultural Commodity Producers," transmitted by the Secretary of Labor to the House Ways and Means and Senate Finance Committees on October 26, 2000. This report was required by Section 408 of the Trade and Development Act of 2000 (P.L. 106-200).

[2] CRS Report RS21182, *Trade Adjustment Assistance for Farmers*, by Geoffrey S. Becker. This report provides background on the TAA for Firms and TAA for Workers programs, the extent to which agricultural businesses and employees in the agricultural sector took advantage of these programs through FY2000, and the legislative developments that led to TAAF program enactment. For information on the other TAA programs and current issues, see CRS Report RS20210, *Trade Adjustment Assistance for Firms: Economic, Program, and Policy Issues*, by J. F. Hornbeck; CRS Report RL34383, *Trade Adjustment Assistance (TAA) for Workers: Current Issues and Legislation*, by John J. Topoleski; CRS Report RS22718, *Trade Adjustment Assistance for Workers (TAA) and Reemployment Trade Adjustment Assistance (RTAA)*, by John J. Topoleski; CRS Report R40863, *Trade Adjustment Assistance for Communities: The Law and Its Implementation*, by Eugene Boyd; and CRS Report RS22761, *Extending Trade Adjustment Assistance (TAA) to Service Workers: How Many Workers Could Potentially Be Covered?*, by John J. Topoleski.

[3] P.L. 107-210, Sections 141-142, approved August 6, 2002, 116 Stat. 946 (19 U.S.C. 2401 et seq.).

[4] American Recovery and Reinvestment Act of 2009, P.L. 111-5, Sections 1856, 1881-1887, and 1891-1894, approved February 17, 2009, 123 Stat. 115.

[5] Defined as "a cause which is important but not necessarily more important than any other cause."

[6] The 2009 amendments in P.L. 111-5 lowered the degree of impact on specified factors due to increased imports that a producer group had to show from 20% to 15%, and expanded the scope of factors that USDA must look at to determine if a producer group can qualify to participate in the program (i.e., from just one specified in the original 2002 law, to the three now). These appear to address two issues that the General Accountability Office (GAO) had identified as limiting producer participation in the initially authorized TAAF program administered through year-end 2007 (see pp. 2-3 of GAO report cited in footnote 16). One was the difficulty that groups of agricultural producers faced in meeting eligibility criteria (i.e., demonstrating that the price of the commodity produced had declined by at least 20% and that imports contributed importantly to the price decline). Also, many producer groups seeking to be recertified for benefits in a subsequent year saw USDA deny their petitions because of their difficulty in showing that imports of a commodity had further increased and that the increase noticeably contributed to the fall in price.

[7] A producer has the option of instead showing that the county-level price for the commodity on the date a group files a petition has decreased compared to the average county-level price in the preceding three marketing years.

[8] Prior to 2009, a producer had to show (1) the quantity of the commodity that he produced in the most recent year, and that (2) his most recent year's net farm income was less than such income in a previous year, (3) he had met with the Extension Service to obtain information

and technical assistance to help him adjust to import competition, and (4) he did not receive cash benefits under any other TAA program.

[9] The 2009 amendments in P.L. 111-5 redirected the type of benefits an individual producer can receive. While a cash payment previously was based on the automatic application of a formula, the more comprehensive approach in place now requires a producer to tap available technical assistance before he receives payments intended to assist him to implement a business plan to adjust to import competition.

[10] Prior to 2009, an approved producer could receive up to $10,000 in cash benefits in any 12-month period.

[11] For additional information on the new payment limitation rules made by P.L. 110-246, see CRS Report RL34594, *Farm Commodity Programs in the 2008 Farm Bill*, by Jim Monke, pp. 14-18.

[12] An ITC safeguard investigation would be triggered, under Section 202 of the Trade Act of 1974, by a petition filed by an affected party (e.g., trade association or industry group) seeking relief from competition caused by imports that are traded fairly but which cause or threaten to cause injury to a domestic industry. For additional information on this safeguard authority and its use, see CRS Report RL3 1296, *Trade Remedies and Agriculture*, by Geoffrey S. Becker and Charles E. Hanrahan.

[13] The statute that established the TAAF program (the Trade Act of 2002) authorized and appropriated to USDA funds not to exceed $90 million for each of FY2003 through FY2007. Section 1(c) of P.L. 110-89 authorized $9 million in appropriations for the first quarter of FY2008 (through December 31, 2007). No funding was authorized during the remainder of FY2008. Funding for FY2009 became available in mid-May 2009, when the changes made to TAA programs by P.L. 111-5 took effect.

[14] Omnibus Trade Act of 2010, P.L. 111-344, Section 101, approved December 29, 2010.

[15] Sections 1892 and 1893 of P.L. 111-5.

[16] GAO, *Trade Adjustment Assistance: New Program for Farmers Provides Some Assistance, but Has Had Limited Participation and Low Program Expenditures*, at http://gao.gov/products/GAO-07-201, GAO-07-201, December 2006.

[17] OIG, Northeast Region, "Audit Report—Trade Adjustment Assistance for Farmers Program," at http://www.usda.gov/oig/webdocs/50601-03-HY.pdf, Report No. 506-1-3-Hy, June 2007, p. 2; and USDA, *FY2009 Budget Summary and Annual Performance Plan*, p. 27.

[18] *Federal Register*, Department of Agriculture, Foreign Agricultural Service, "Trade Adjustment Assistance for Farmers," August, 25, 2009, pp. 42799-42804, available at http://edocket.access

[19] *Federal Register*, Department of Agriculture, Foreign Agricultural Service, "Trade Adjustment Assistance for Farmers," March 1, 2010, pp. 9087-9093, available at http://edocket.access and March 11, 2010, p. 11513, available at http://edocket.access.gpo.gov/2010/pdf/2010-5238.pdf.

[20] For more information, see CRS Report RL33663, *Generalized System of Preferences: Background and Renewal Debate*, by Vivian C. Jones.

[21] For more information, see CRS Report RS22548, *ATPA Renewal: Background and Issues*, by M. Angeles Villarreal.

[22] *Washington Trade Daily*, "Tying TAA, ATPA to the FTAs," February 9, 2011, p. 1; *Inside U.S. Trade*, "ATPDEA, TAA Extensions Likely Deadlocked, Business Worries About Fallout," February 11, 2010, pp. 1, 15.

In: Global Competition
Editors: Dianna J. Hall et al.
ISBN: 978-1-61324-712-9

Chapter 3

TRADE ADJUSTMENT ASSISTANCE FOR WORKERS (TAA) AND REEMPLOYMENT TRADE ADJUSTMENT ASSISTANCE (RTAA)

John J. Topoleski

SUMMARY

Trade Adjustment Assistance for Workers (TAA) provides assistance to qualifying workers who lose their jobs directly due to increased imports or shifts in production out of the United States. Certified workers whose unemployment compensation has ended and who are in approved training may receive income support payments (Trade Readjustment Allowances, or TRA) for a maximum of 156 weeks. Some workers age 50 or older are eligible to receive Reemployment Trade Adjustment Assistance (RTAA), a wage supplement program. Both TAA- and RTAA-eligible workers can receive a Health Coverage Tax Credit (HCTC), which provides a refundable tax credit to offset 80% of the health insurance premiums of TAA- and RTAA-eligible workers. This report provides background on the programs, including a description of the eligibility for these programs and benefits available to participants. It also describes the main changes to the program with the reauthorization and expansion of TAA in the American Recovery and Reinvestment Act of 2009 (ARRA; P.L. 111-5), which was signed into law by President Barack Obama on February 17, 2009. The changes made by ARRA were to expire on December 31, 2010. H.R. 6517, the Omnibus Trade Act of

2010, extended the changes made by ARRA though February 12, 2011. H.R. 6517 passed the House and the Senate on December 22, 2010.

Background

Trade Adjustment Assistance for Workers (TAA) provides extended income support as well as training, job search, and relocation benefits.[1] To be eligible for TAA, workers must have become unemployed for one of three reasons: (1) their jobs moved to another country; (2) their job losses can be attributed to increased imports that contributed importantly to an actual decline in sales or production; or (3) their job losses resulted from the loss of business with a primary firm because of a trade-related reason. Older TAA-eligible workers may be able to opt for Reemployment Trade Adjustment Assistance (RTAA), which provides a wage supplement in lieu of TAA benefits. In addition, workers can claim a refundable Health Coverage Tax Credit (HCTC). The HCTC was established to help both eligible TAA and RTAA workers pay for health insurance.[2]

TAA was formally established by the Trade Expansion Act of 1962 (P.L. 87-794) but was little used until the Trade Act of 1974 (P.L. 93-618) expanded benefits and eligibility. Most recently, the Trade Act of 2002 (P.L. 107-210) established RTAA and reauthorized and expanded TAA. TAA and RTAA were set to expire December 31, 2007. The House passed a three-month extension (H.R. 4341) by a voice vote. However, the Senate did not act on the measure. The Consolidated Appropriations Act, 2008 (P.L. 110-161, signed by President George W. Bush on December 26, 2007) contained an appropriation for the TAA for Workers and RTAA programs that fully funded the programs for FY2008.[3] The Consolidated Security, Disaster Assistance, and Continuing Appropriations Act, 2009 (P.L. 110-329) fully funds the TAA and RTAA programs through March 6, 2009, and specified that the programs will continue through this date. The American Recovery and Reinvestment Act of 2009 (ARRA; P.L. 111-5, which was signed into law by President Barack Obama on February 17, 2009) reauthorized and expanded TAA. Authorization for the changes made by ARRA were set to expire on December 31, 2010. H.R. 6517, the Omnibus Trade Act of 2010, extended the changes made by ARRA though February 12, 2011. H.R. 6517 passed the House and the Senate on December 22, 2010.

FINANCING

TAA financing has several components. Trade Readjustment Allowances (TRA) funds for extended unemployment benefits are appropriated as an entitlement out of general revenue (not out of the Unemployment Trust Fund). TRA benefits are provided to all workers who meet eligibility requirements. In FY2010, $1.1 billion was appropriated for TRA benefits. Funds for training, job search and relocation expenses, and administrative costs are a line item appropriation of which training is a capped entitlement. The TAA statute authorizes $575 million for training. The RTAA is appropriated as an entitlement out of the general fund. In FY2010, $65.0 million was appropriated for RTAA. HCTC is funded out of general revenue.

ADMINISTRATION

At the federal level, the TAA and RTAA programs are administered by the Office of Trade Adjustment Assistance within the U.S. Department of Labor (DOL). Claims for benefits by individual workers are administered by the state Unemployment Compensation (UC) agencies under agreements and contracts with DOL. The use of funds varies greatly from year to year and from state to state.

TRADE ADJUSTMENT ASSISTANCE BENEFITS

TAA benefits, which are primarily focused on the re-employment of certified workers, have several components: up to 156 weeks of income support while in training; training assistance; and job search and relocation assistance.

Income Support (Trade Readjustment Allowances)

Workers have both basic and additional TRA available to them and can receive up to 156 weeks of income support.

- **Basic TRA.** Workers receive basic TRA after their UC benefits are exhausted. The weekly TRA payment is equal to the worker's most recent UC benefit. The total amount of basic TRA benefits available to a worker is equal to 52 times the weekly TRA benefit minus the total amount of UC benefits. For example, a worker who receives 26 weeks of UC would be eligible to receive an additional 26 weeks of basic TRA.[4] To receive the basic TRA benefit, workers must be enrolled or participating in TAA-approved training, have completed such training, or have obtained a waiver of the training requirement.[5]
- **Additional TRA.** An additional 78 weeks of income support is available for workers who are enrolled in TAA-approved training programs, plus another 26 weeks are available for workers in remedial training programs. A worker cannot receive a waiver of the training requirement to receive additional TRA.

Training Assistance

Workers' training assistance is for full-time participation in an approved training program. Approved training programs include, but are not limited to, employer-based training, including customized training and on-the-job training; any training program provided by a state pursuant to Title I of the Workforce Investment Act of 1998 (WIA; P.L. 105-220); any training program approved by a private industry council under Section 102 of WIA; a program of prerequisite education; a training program or coursework at an accredited higher education institution; or any training program for which all, or any portion, of the costs are paid (1) under a federal or state program or (2) from any other source. According to DOL, between July 2006 and June 2007 the average number of weeks of training per participant was 63, and 72% of participants completed training.

Job Search and Relocation Assistance

Certified workers who cannot obtain suitable employment within their commuting areas can receive an allowance of 100% of their job search and relocation expenses, up to a maximum of $1,500 for each benefit. Less than 1% of TAA-eligible workers receive these benefits.

- **Job Search Allowance.** Applications must be submitted before a job search begins and made by the 365th day after certification or final separation (whichever is later) or within 182 days of the end of training.
- **Relocation Expenses.** Applications must be submitted before the relocation occurs and made within 425 days of certification or layoff (whichever is later) or within 182 days of the end of training. The relocation must occur within 182 days of filing the application for relocation assistance or within 182 days after the conclusion of training.

REEMPLOYMENT TRADE ADJUSTMENT ASSISTANCE BENEFITS

Workers who qualify for the RTAA benefit can receive a wage supplement worth half the difference in salary between their old and new jobs for a maximum of $12,000 over two years. Although workers are ineligible if their wages are more than $55,000 a year, their combined wages and RTAA payments can exceed $55,000 a year. For example, a worker who earned $58,000 at a previous job and earns $53,000 at a new job would be eligible for a benefit of $2,500 per year for two years. In this case, the worker would receive a total of $55,500 per year (for two years) in wages and RTAA benefits.

HEALTH COVERAGE TAX CREDIT BENEFIT

HCTC is available to TAA and RTAA workers. The HCTC covers 80% of the premium for qualified health insurance purchased by an eligible taxpayer (the taxpayer is responsible for the other 20%). It is refundable, so workers may claim the full credit even if they have little or no federal income tax liability. The credit may also be advanced, so taxpayers have the option of using the credit on a monthly basis when premiums are due rather than waiting until the end of the year. Individuals may receive the HCTC for one month longer than their TAA eligibility or exactly two years in the case of their RTAA eligibility.

ELIGIBILITY

Obtaining TAA or RTAA benefits is a two-stage process: (1) a group of workers must petition DOL to become TAA certified. A group of workers that is TAA certified is automatically certified for RTAA; and (2) individual workers apply for TAA or RTAA benefits at a local One-Stop Career Center.

TAA Group Eligibility

To gain TAA eligibility, a group of three or more workers (or their union, firm, or state) petitions DOL. Then, DOL investigates whether import competition "contributed importantly" to the group's job loss or whether their firm has shifted their jobs to a foreign country. TAA also extends eligibility to groups of secondary workers whose job losses result from the loss of business with a primary firm (i.e., the firm that directly lost business or outsourced as a result of trade).

Certification of the petition requires that firms meet one of several criteria.

In the case of a firm that shifts production to a foreign country, certification requires the following:

- A significant number of workers[6] are laid off or threatened with layoffs;
- Either (1) a shift in the production of articles or services like or directly competitive with those produced by the workers' firm to a foreign country, or (2) the workers' firm has acquired the articles or services from a foreign country; and
- The shift in production or acquisition of foreign goods or services contributed importantly to the workers' separation.

In the case of a firm that does not shift production to a foreign country, certification requires the following:

- A significant number of workers are laid off or threatened with layoffs;
- The sales or production of the firm decreased; and
- Increased imports of (1) articles or services competitive with the firm's articles or service or (2) articles which are competitive with the

articles in which the firm's products or services are component parts or services have "contributed importantly" to the decline in sales or production.

In the case of public sector workers, certification requires the following:

- A significant number of workers in the public agency are laid off or threatened with layoffs;
- The public agency has acquired like or competitive services from a foreign country, and
- The acquisition of the services contributed importantly to the workers' separation.

In the case of adversely affected secondary workers, certification requires the following:

- A significant number of workers are laid off or threatened with layoffs;
- The workers' firm is a supplier or downstream producer to a TAA-certified firm; and;
- Either (1) the sales or production to the TAA-certified firm accounted for at least 20% of the sales or production of the supplier firm or (2) the loss of sales to the TAA-certified firm contributed importantly to the workers' job losses.

The determination on a TAA petition must be made by DOL within 40 days of filing. Generally, the certification covers all members of the worker group who are laid off during the three-year period beginning one year before the petition was filed (the *impact date*) and ending two years after the date of the certification. Determinations on TAA petitions are published in the Federal Register and on the DOL website. Workers who are denied certification may request administrative reconsideration by DOL. Reconsideration requests must be mailed within 30 days of Federal Register publication. Workers who are denied certification may seek judicial review of DOL's initial petition denial or denial following administrative reconsideration. Appeals for judicial review must be filed with U.S. Court of International Trade within 60 days of Federal Register publication of the initial denial or administrative reconsideration denial.

TAA Individual Eligibility

If DOL certifies a petitioner's group of workers as eligible, the individual workers then apply to their state agency to establish a TAA benefit claim. For an individual worker, eligibility is based on all of the following: (1) separation from the firm on or after the impact date specified in the certification but within two years of DOL certification; (2) employment with the affected firm in at least 26 of the 52 weeks preceding layoff; (3) entitlement to state UC benefits; (4) no disqualification for extended unemployment benefits; and (5) enrollment or a waiver for participation in an approved training program. Certified workers who are denied individual benefits can appeal the decision. The determination notice that certified workers receive after filing their applications for each benefit will explain their appeal rights and time limits for filing appeals.

RTAA Group Eligibility

A group of workers certified for TAA eligibility are eligible for RTAA as well. Neither separate petitions nor separate certifications are required for RTAA.

RTAA Individual Eligibility

If DOL certifies a group as TAA and RTAA eligible, then an individual worker must meet the following requirements:

- be at least 50 years old at the time of reemployment and
- obtain full-time employment earning less than $55,000 per year by sooner of the exhaustion of unemployment compensation or during any point in which the worker is receiving TRA. This allows a worker to shift from receiving TRA to receiving RTAA.

Table 1. Petitions and Certifications, FY2003-FY2009.

	Petitions Filed		Petitions Certified		
Fiscal Year	Petitions	Estimated Workers	Number	Percentage	Estimated Workers
2003	3,567	292,827	1,880	53%	197,359
2004	2,992	171,281	1,802	60%	149,705
2005	2,638	164,371	1,534	58%	118,022
2006	2,478	172,651	1,426	57%	119,602
2007	2,228	190,430	1,427	64%	146,606
2008	2,146	162,629	1,368	64%	125,529
2009	2,295	243,208	1,844	80%	201,094

Source: CRS table from data provided by the U.S. Department of Labor, Employment and Training Administration.

Table 2. Selected Statistics on TAA Benefits, FY2003-FY2009.

	Trade Readjustment Allowance			Training, Job Search, Relocation Allowances			
Fiscal Year	New Recipients of Basic TRA	Average Weekly Basic TRA Payment ($)	Total TRA Outlays ($millions)	Entered Training	Job Search	Re-location	Total Outlays ($ millions)
2003	44,000	238	352	44,000	430	736	259
2004	81,000	262	530	51,000	467	817	259
2005	55,000	267	598	38,000	288	446	259
2006	53,000	289	529	37,000	454	531	259
2007	47,000	329	572	44,000	399	750	259
2008	42,000	310	509	38,000	405	757	259
2009	na	na	na	58,000	617	682	259

Source: Table provided to CRS by U.S. Department of Labor, Employment and Training Administration.

Note: na indicates that data are not available.

PARTICIPATION

Table 1 includes data on TAA petitions and certifications for FY2003 to FY2009. The numbers do not exhibit a particular trend over time because the number of petitions depends on the episodic nature of layoffs, especially within a particular state.[7] Factors that could explain the increase in petitions and certifications in FY2009 include the recession beginning in December 2007 and the expansion of TAA eligibility beginning in May 2009.

Table 2 includes data on TAA benefits for FY2003 to FY2009. The number of new recipients of basic TRA has declined each year since 2004. The reporting requirements were changed beginning in FY2007, therefore, FY2007 and FY2008 data for number of workers who entered training may not be comparable to previous years.

In FY2009, a total amount of $19 million was received by 6,827 participants in RTAA wage supplement program.

CHANGES TO TAA DUE TO REAUTHORIZATION

The American Recovery and Reinvestment Act of 2009 (ARRA, P.L. 111-5) reauthorized and expanded TAA and was signed into law by President Barack Obama on February 17, 2009. The act went into effect May 18, 2009, which was 90 days after enactment. The provisions enacted by ARRA are as follows:

- Extended TAA eligibility to service and public sector workers. Prior law required that workers produce an article to be eligible for TAA.
- Extended TAA eligibility to suppliers of component parts if the supplier experiences job losses for a trade-related reason regardless of whether the downstream producer is a TAA-certified firm. Prior law allowed suppliers of component parts to be certified for TAA only if the downstream producer was certified for TAA.
- Allowed TAA eligibility due to shifts in production to any country. Prior law required that firms shift production to countries with which the United States has a free-trade or beneficial trading agreement.
- Allowed workers to receive Additional TRA (income support payments) for an additional 26 weeks (for a total of 78 weeks), provided the workers are in training. Prior law allowed workers to receive Additional TRA for up to 52 weeks, provided the workers were in training.
- Extended the deadline for enrolling in training to the later of 26 weeks from the date of TAA certification or the date of separation from employment. Prior law required workers to enroll in training the later

of 8 weeks after TAA certification or 16 weeks after separation from employment.

- Increased training funding to $575 million per fiscal year. Prior law authorized $220 million per fiscal year for workers' training.
- Required DOL to disburse training funds to states based on at least five factors; distribute at least 65% of the training funds in the initial distribution; and to disburse to a state no less than 25% of the prior year's initial distribution. Prior law did not specify any method for training funds to be allocated to states. In practice, DOL initially disbursed 75% of training funds based on a state's accrued training expenditures and the number of training participants over the previous two and one-half years, and disbursed to a state no less than 85% of the prior year's initial distribution.
- Increased the amount reimbursed for job search and relocation expenses to 100% of a worker's expenses up to $1,500 for each type of expense. Prior law limited reimbursement for job search and relocation expenses to 90% of a worker's expenses up to $1,250 for each type of expense.
- Continued the wage insurance program for older workers as RTAA. Prior law established Alternative Trade Adjustment Assistance (ATAA) for older workers as a five-year demonstration project.
- Eliminated the separate petition process for eligibility for the wage insurance program. Prior law required a separate ATAA petition to be filed concurrently with the TAA petition.
- Allowed older workers to be eligible for RTAA for up to two years after the exhaustion of regular unemployment benefits or reemployment. The new law allowed workers participating in TAA-approved training to receive wage insurance if they switch from receiving TRA while in training to receiving RTAA. Prior law required workers to find reemployment within 26 weeks of separation and also prohibited workers who receive TRA from receiving wage insurance.
- Increased the limit on wages to be eligible for reemployment assistance to $55,000 per year and increased the maximum wage insurance benefit to $12,000 over two years. Prior law limited eligibility to workers with reemployment wages less than $50,000 and limited the maximum benefit to $10,000 over two years.
- Established an Office of Trade Adjustment Assistance in DOL to be headed by an administrator who will report directly to the Deputy

Assistant Director for Employment and Training. Under prior law, TAA was administered as part of the Office of National Response.

- Increased the HCTC to 80% of a worker's qualified health insurance premiums beginning April 18, 2009. Prior law covered 65% of a worker's qualified health insurance premiums.
- Authorized TAA and RTAA through December 31, 2010. H.R. 6517, which passed the House and Senate on December 22, 2010, extended the TAA program as expanded by ARRA through February 12, 2011.

Expiration of TAA Expansions under ARRA

The provisions in ARRA that expanded benefit eligibility under the TAA program were scheduled to sunset on December 31, 2010. In addition, ARRA provided that on January 1, 2011, the TAA program be administered as if the provisions of ARRA had not been enacted, although workers covered by petitions filed before January 1, 2011, would receive benefits under the TAA program as expanded by ARRA. Finally, ARRA provided that the authorization for the TAA program would expire on December 31, 2011.

H.R. 6517, the Omnibus Trade Act of 2010, extended the provisions of the TAA program as enacted by ARRA though February 12, 2011. H.R. 6517 passed the House and the Senate on December 22, 2010, and was signed by President Barack Obama on December 29, 2010.

End Notes

[1] Other Trade Adjustment Assistance available is TAA for Firms (see CRS Report RS20210, *Trade Adjustment Assistance for Firms: Economic, Program, and Policy Issues*, by J. F. Hornbeck), and TAA for Farmers (see CRS Report R40206, *Trade Adjustment Assistance for Farmers*, by Remy Jurenas).

[2] For more information, see CRS Report RL32620, *Health Coverage Tax Credit*, by Bernadette Fernandez.

[3] For more information see CRS Report RL34383, *Trade Adjustment Assistance (TAA) for Workers: Current Issues and Legislation*, by John J. Topoleski.

[4] Amounts of Emergency Unemployment Compensation or Extended Benefits (EB) offset the amount of Basic TRA for which a worker is eligible. For example, a worker that receives 13 weeks of EB in addition to the usual 26 weeks of UC would be entitled to receive 13 weeks of Basic TRA.

[5] Reasons for a training waiver include the following: the worker will be recalled reasonably soon, the worker has marketable skills for suitable employment and a reasonable expectation of employment, the worker is within two years of eligibility for a pension or Social Security, the worker is unable to participate in or complete training for health

reasons, the worker cannot enroll in training immediately, or the worker cannot find a suitable training program.

[6] DOL regulations (see 20 C.F.R. § 90.2) define *significant* to mean that the group of workers must contain at least 3 workers if the firm had less than 50 workers, or 5% of total workers if the firm had 50 or more workers.

[7] For example, the Government Accountability Office notes that Kansas had 4,117 trade-affected workers laid off in 2004, 75 in 2006, and 721 in 2007. See GAO-07-994T, *Trade Adjustment Assistance: Program Provides an Array of Benefits and Services to Trade-Affected Workers*, June 14, 2007, available at http://www.gao.gov/new.items/ d07995t.pdf.

In: Global Competition
Editors: Dianna J. Hall et al.
ISBN: 978-1-61324-712-9

Chapter 4

EXTENDING TRADE ADJUSTMENT ASSISTANCE (TAA) TO SERVICE WORKERS: HOW MANY WORKERS COULD POTENTIALLY BE COVERED?

John J. Topoleski

SUMMARY

Trade Adjustment Assistance (TAA) provides income support and training assistance to workers who become unemployed for certain trade-related reasons. Only workers who make an article (i.e., manufacturing workers) are eligible for TAA. Under current law, service workers who become unemployed for a trade-related reason (e.g., outsourcing) are ineligible for TAA. Several bills in the 110th Congress (S. 1848, H.R. 910, H.R. 3589, H.R. 3920) would expand TAA to include service workers and public sector employees. The available data indicates that the number of displaced *manufacturing* workers in offshorable occupations from 2003 to 2005 (489,000) roughly equals the number of TAA-certified manufacturing workers over the same period (450,000). There were 840,000 workers displaced from offshorable *nonmanufacturing* occupations from 2003 to 2005, suggesting that the pool of TAA-eligible workers could have increased by over 170% if service workers had been eligible for TAA. In January 2006, nearly three times as many employed nonmanufacturing workers were in offshorable occupations (20.7 million) than employed manufacturing workers in offshorable occupations (7.7 million), suggesting a large increase in the pool of potentially eligible TAA workers.

TAA Background

TAA provides income support and training assistance to certain workers who lose their jobs for a trade-related reason. For example, manufacturing workers who are laid off either due to a company shifting production to a country with which the United States has a free trade agreement or a manufacturing company switching to a supplier in any foreign country would be eligible for TAA. Manufacturing workers who lose their jobs due to a general economic decline are not eligible for TAA. TAA was most recently reauthorized by the Trade Act of 2002 (P.L. 107-210) and was set to expire on September 30, 2007. P.L. 110-89 extended TAA until December 31, 2007. P.L. 110-161, signed on December 26, 2007, fully funds TAA through September 30, 2008. The Department of Labor has indicated that this is sufficient to continue the program, including issuing new certifications of eligible workers.[1]

Currently, TAA eligibility is generally limited to workers in firms that make an article, which excludes most nonmanufacturing workers in the United States. In the 110th Congress, several bills (S. 1848, H.R. 910, H.R. 3589, H.R. 3920) would expand TAA eligibility. For example, S. 1848 and H.R. 3920 would extend TAA to workers in service sector firms or public agencies. The bills also eliminate the requirement that the shift in production be to a country with which the United States has a free-trade agreement. So, for example, workers whose jobs are "offshored" to any country regardless of whether they produce a product or a service would be eligible for TAA under S. 1848 and H.R. 3920.[2]

TAA Benefits and Financing

TAA has two primary benefits: Trade Readjustment Allowances (TRA) and training, job search, and relocation benefits.

TRA provides up to 130 weeks of income support if a TAA-eligible worker is participating in an approved training program. TRA is a mandatory spending program. Because TRA benefits are provided to all who meet the eligibility requirements, under current financing provisions, no workers would lose TRA income support benefits if there were an increase in the pool of TAA eligible workers. An increase in TRA expenditures would be paid for — like all mandatory funding — through some combination of borrowing, increased revenues, or spending cuts.

In contrast to TRA, the training, job search, and relocation assistance aspect of TAA is a capped entitlement. The Trade Act of 2002 specifically limits training expenditures to $220 million per fiscal year. In FY2007, an additional $39 million was appropriated for job search and relocation expenses. S. 1848 would increase the amount of training funds to $440 million in FY2008 and increase the annual appropriation by 10% if states had obligated or expended 90% of the previous year's authorization. H.R. 3920 would increase training funds to $440 million in FY2008 and FY2009 and $660 million in each fiscal year thereafter. An expansion of TAA to include service workers might present additional challenges to the management of training funds. TAA funds are allocated to states on the basis of worker participation and expenditures for the prior two and a half years. However, a state that experiences unexpectedly large layoffs might find training funds insufficient to meet the demand and so have to ration the available training funds. Both S. 1848 and H.R. 3920 adjust the funding formula used to allocate training funds to address these funding concerns.

IMPACT

To examine the impact of offshoring on the number of potential TAA-eligible workers, this report examines workers in occupations that have the potential to be offshored. The report examines the offshorability of displaced or employed workers' occupations and categorizes the number of workers, first, by the offshorable potential of their occupations and, second, by whether the workers are employed in the manufacturing, nonmanufacturing, or government sectors. The report analyzes two sets of data: (1) long-tenured displaced workers from January 2003 to December 2005 and (2) workers who were employed in January 2006.

Data

This report uses employment data from the Current Population Survey (CPS). The CPS is a monthly survey of about 50,000 households conducted by the Bureau of the Census for the Bureau of Labor Statistics (BLS) and is the primary source of information on the labor force characteristics of the U.S. population. We use the January 2006 CPS to examine the number of workers employed in January 2006. In addition, this report also uses the Displaced Workers Survey (DWS), a supplement to the January CPS in even years. The January 2006 DWS provides information on workers who were displaced from their jobs between January 2003 and December 2005. This report does not include agriculture workers and members of the armed forces.

Variable Definitions

To determine which occupations were potentially offshorable, this report uses a list created by Princeton University economist and former Vice Chairman of the Board of Governors of the Federal Reserve System Alan S. Blinder.[3] Blinder classifies occupations as "highly offshorable," "offshorable," "non-offshorable," or "highly non-offshorable" on the basis of the occupation's description in the Department of Labor's O*NET database. By offshoring, Blinder means "the migration of employment from the U.S. and other rich countries to other (mostly poorer) countries."

Conforming to the BLS definition of manufacturing occupations, this report uses occupations listed as Production Occupations by the Census Bureau. Government workers may be from any occupation but are employed by a local, state, or federal government.

Displaced workers are persons 20 years of age and older who lost or left jobs because their plants or companies closed or moved, there was insufficient work for them to do, or their positions or shifts were abolished. This report uses the BLS definition of "long- tenured" displaced workers. These are workers who had worked for their employers for three or more years at the time of displacement. Whereas TAA eligibility only requires that a worker be employed at the firm for 26 of the 52 weeks preceding the layoff, using long-tenured workers may better approximate the number of TAA-eligible workers. Although this likely slightly underestimates the number of TAA-eligible workers, using all displaced workers, including "short-tenured" would likely greatly overestimate TAA-eligible workers. Support for using "long-tenured" displaced workers can be found in a recent Government Accountability Office (GAO) report that found 91.7% of TAA-eligible workers from five plant closings had been at their place of employment for at least five years.[4]

CAVEATS

This methodology may overestimate or underestimate the number of workers whose jobs are outsourced and who would potentially be eligible for TAA. Unfortunately, neither the Census Bureau nor BLS collects data on the number of jobs that have been offshored. Some important caveats include the following.

- Not all job losses in the "highly offshorable" or "offshorable" categories would be eligible for TAA as it currently exists or as it might be expanded to service workers. For example, it is entirely possible for workers in a manufacturing plant in an "offshorable" occupation to lose their jobs because of a plant fire or a general downturn in the economy. Such workers would not be eligible for TAA.
- The estimates in this report represent a sort of upper limit on the number of workers potentially eligible for TAA. An assumption is that workers in non-offshorable or highly non-offshorable occupations will not lose their jobs to offshoring. A worker in a non-offshorable occupation may be offshored in the future, particularly if technology changes the nature of work in an occupation.
- Blinder's list is of "potentially offshorable occupations." It makes no prediction as to the actual number of jobs that will be offshored. Blinder rates the ease with which a job could be offshored on the basis of the job description. For example, the physical presence required by janitorial staff suggests a lower probability of being offshored than call-center workers who could perform their jobs from any location.
- It would be very difficult to predict the number of nonmanufacturing job losses that would be eligible for TAA. Although it appears that the number of displaced manufacturing workers in highly-offshorable and offshorable categories closely matches the number of workers on petitions that were TAA certified, this may or may not be the case

with nonmanufacturing and government workers. Therefore, extrapolating to the nonmanufacturing sector is difficult.

- This report does not calculate standard errors. Therefore, the difference between manufacturing and nonmanufacturing workers may or may not be statistically significant (i.e., the results could be due to chance).

RESULTS

Generally, the results show manufacturing occupations have a much greater *percentage* of offshorable employed and displaced workers than private non-manufacturing occupations but that the *number* of private nonmanufacturing offshorable employed and displaced workers is considerably higher than manufacturing workers. As a group, manufacturing occupations are more likely to be (or to have been) offshored, but there are many more nonmanufacturing employed and displaced workers in offshorable occupations. If proposed legislation were enacted, the pool of potentially TAA-eligible workers could increase anywhere from two to four times the current number.

Table 1 indicates the number of potentially offshorable, long-tenured displaced workers within three major categories of occupations: Private Nonmanufacturing, Government, and Production.

There were 3.8 million displaced workers from 2003 to 2005, of which 1.4 million (36%) were in potentially offshorable positions.

- Nearly all (93%) displaced production workers were in offshorable occupations. In contrast, only 28% of private, nonmanufacturing displaced workers were in offshorable occupations. Finally, only 12% of displaced government workers were in offshorable occupations.
- Nearly two-thirds of displaced workers in offshorable occupations were from nonmanufacturing and government occupations. These displaced workers would not have been eligible for TAA under current law, but might be under proposed legislation.
- There were 489,000 displaced production workers in offshorable occupations. For comparison, there were 446,000 workers certified for TAA from 2003 to 2005.

Table 1. Number of Long-Tenured Displaced Workers by Potential Offshorability of Occupation.

Occupation Category	Highly Offshorable	Offshorable	Total of Both Highly Offshorable and Offshorable	Non-Offshorable	Highly Non-Offshorable	Total
Total Private	385,042	452,689	**837,736**	504,954	1,704,175	3,046,861
Nonmanufacturing	(12.6%)	(14.9%)	**(27.5%)**	(16.6%)	(55.9%)	(100.0%)
Government	11,594 (5.7%)	13,736 (6.7%)	**25,330** **(12.4%)**	21,446 (10.5%)	158,269 (77.2%)	205,045 (100.0%)
Production	60,749	428,238	**488,986**	23,579	11,379	523,944
(Manufacturing)	(11.6%)	(81.7%)	**(93.3%)**	(4.5%)	(2.2%)	(100.0%)
Total	457,385 (12.1%)	894,663 (23.7%)	**1,352,048** **(35.8%)**	549,979 (14.6%)	1,873,823 (49.6%)	3,775,850 (100.0%)

Source: CRS calculations from the January 2006 Displaced Workers Survey refer to workers who were displaced from their jobs between January 2003 and December 2005. We use Alan Blinder's definitions of offshorability.

Note: For emphasis, the bolded column combines the workers in the highly offshorable and offshorable categories.

The four categories of offshorability sum to 100% (shown in the last column).

Table 2. Number of Employed Persons in the United States as of January 2006 by Potential Offshorability of Occupation.

Occupation Category	Highly Offshorable	Offshorable	Total of Both Highly Offshorable and Offshorable	Non-Offshorable	Highly Non-Offshorable	Total
Total Private	9,047,153	11,663,215	**20,710,368**	12,329,994	68,103,345	101,143,707
Nonmanufacturing	(8.9%)	(11.5%)	**(20.5%)**	(12.2%)	(67.3%)	(100.0%)
Government	1,146,632 (5.7%)	2,163,486 (10.8%)	**3,310,118** **(16.6%)**	2,060,678 (10.3%)	14,599,462 (73.1%)	19,970,259 (100.0%)
Production	508,106	7,212,651	**7,720,757**	287,952	795,611	8,804,319
(Manufacturing)	(5.8%)	(81.9%)	**(87.7%)**	(337%)	(9.0%)	(100.0%)
Total	10,701,892 (5.2%)	21,039,352 (16.2%)	**31,741,244** **(24.5%)**	14,678,624 (11.3%)	85,353,928 (64.2%)	129,918,285 (100.0%)

Source: CRS calculations from the January 2006 Current Population Survey. We use Alan Blinder's definitions of offshorability.

Note: For emphasis, the bolded column combines the workers in the highly offshorable and offshorable categories. The four categories of offshorability sum to 100% (shown in the last column).

- Most nonmanufacturing occupations are non-offshorable, although within private, nonmanufacturing occupation categories there is considerable variation in offshorable potential. For example, although 100% of legal occupations are considered offshorable, only 7% of information occupations are potentially offshorable.
- Had displaced nonmanufacturing workers been eligible for TAA from 2003 to 2005, the number of TAA-eligible workers potentially could have more than doubled from 490,000 to 1.4 million.

Table 2 contains data on the number of workers employed in January 2006.

- There were 32 million (24.5%) workers employed in offshorable occupations.
- For most employment categories, the percentage of potentially offshorable current workers is less than the percentage of displaced workers in offshorable occupations. For example, 20.5% of *employed* nonmanufacturing workers are in potentially offshorable occupations (from Table 2) compared with 27.5% of *displaced* nonmanufacturing workers (from Table 1).
- Although there were 1.7 times as many displaced private, *nonmanufacturing* workers as displaced *manufacturing* workers (from Table 1), there were 2.7 times as many private, nonmanufacturing workers employed in offshorable occupations in January 2006. If government sector workers are included, this suggests that the pool of potentially TAA-eligible workers could more than quadruple from 7.7 million to 31.7 million in the future if TAA is expanded to include service and government sector employees.

End Notes

[1] For more information see CRS Report RS227 18, *Trade Adjustment Assistance for Workers (TAA) and Alternative Trade Adjustment Assistance for Older Workers (ATAA),* by John J. Topoleski.

[2] For more information on offshoring see CRS Report RL32292, *Offshoring (a.k.a. Offshore Outsourcing) and Job Insecurity Among U.S. Workers*, by Linda Levine.

[3] See Alan S. Blinder, *How Many U.S. Jobs Might Be Offshorable?,* CEPS Working Paper No. 142, March 2007, available at [http://www.princeton.edu/~blinder/papers/07ceps142.pdf].

[4] GAO-06-43, *Trade Adjustment Assistance: Most Workers in Five Layoffs Received Services, but Better Outreach Needed on New Benefits*, available at [http://www.gao.gov/new.items/d0643 .pdf].

In: Global Competition
Editors: Dianna J. Hall et al.
ISBN: 978-1-61324-712-9

Chapter 5

TRADE ADJUSTMENT ASSISTANCE PROGRAM PROVIDES AN ARRAY OF BENEFITS AND SERVICES TO TRADE-AFFECTED WORKERS

United States Government Accountability Office

WHY GAO DID THIS STUDY

Manufacturing workers face an uncertain future as manufacturing employment declines—more than 3 million manufacturing jobs have been lost in this country since 2000, many due to international trade. Furthermore, finding a new job may be harder for these workers because they tend to be older with have fewer transferable skills than other laid-off workers. The Trade Adjustment Assistance (TAA) program was established in 1962 to assist manufacturing workers who lose their jobs because of international trade. In 2002, the Congress made a number of key changes designed to expand benefits and decrease the time it takes to get workers into services. This testimony draws upon several GAO reports, including our most recently issued TAA report and our case study of five layoffs, and provides an overview of (1) how the TAA program operates, (2) recent trends in the Department of Labor's (Labor) certification of petitions, (3) the extent to which workers participate in training, (4) the extent to which workers take advantage of other TAA benefits, and (5) what is known about TAA program outcomes.

We are not making new recommendations at this time. Labor generally agreed with the findings and recommendations in our referenced reports.

WHAT GAO FOUND

The process for enrolling trade-affected workers in the TAA program begins when a petition for TAA assistance is filed with Labor on behalf of a group of workers. Labor has generally processed these petitions in a timely manner, taking on average 32 days during the past 3 fiscal years. Once enrolled, trade-affected workers can access a variety of TAA benefits and services, including income support, job training, and health coverage. Workers typically access these services through one-stop centers where they also receive case management services, such as counseling and vocational assessments.

During the past 3 fiscal years, the number of petitions certified and the number of petitions filed have declined. The proportion of petitions certified has remained relatively stable, as Labor certified about two-thirds of petitions investigated in each of these years. These petitions covered an estimated 400,000 workers. Petitions were most commonly denied because workers were not involved in the production of articles, a basic requirement of the TAA program.

Nationally, the decline in the number of workers entering training from fiscal years 2004 to 2006 parallels a decline in the estimated number of trade-affected workers. However, there are wide state-to-state variations in this trend. Sixteen states reported a decrease in training enrollment during the past 3 fiscal years, while 20 states reported an increase.

We also found that few TAA participants take advantage of the wage insurance and health coverage benefits. Although the number of new workers receiving the wage insurance benefit has increased from 1,400 in 2004, to about 3,200 in 2006, the number remains small—two-thirds of the states estimate that 5 percent or less of their TAA participants received wage insurance in fiscal year 2006. Participation in the health coverage benefit is also low. Approximately 6,900 workers enrolled for the first time in the advance health coverage benefit in fiscal year 2006.

Finally, we found that the nationwide TAA performance data that are currently available do not provide a complete and credible picture of the program's performance. However, at our five case study sites, we found that most of the workers who lost their jobs because of foreign trade had either found a job or retired at the time of our survey. The majority of reemployed workers earned less in their new jobs than they had previously earned, but generally replaced about 80 percent or more of their pre-layoff wages.

Mr. Chairman and Members of the Committee:

We are pleased to have the opportunity to discuss the assistance available through the Trade Adjustment Assistance (TAA) program to workers who are dislocated because of international trade. We have conducted a number of studies on the TAA program since the program was last reauthorized in 2002, and this testimony will focus primarily on the results of that work. [1]

Manufacturing workers face an uncertain future as manufacturing employment declines—more than 3 million manufacturing jobs have been lost in this country since 2000, many due to international trade. Furthermore, finding a new job may be harder for these workers because they tend to be older, with fewer transferable skills than other laid-off workers. To assist these workers, the Congress established the TAA program in 1962 to provide income support, job training, and other benefits for manufacturing workers who lose their jobs as a result of international trade. TAA, administered by the Department of Labor (Labor), was funded at about $900 million in fiscal year 2006, including $220 million for training. In 2002, the Congress made a number of key changes designed to expand benefits and decrease the time it takes to get workers into services. Among the changes, the act

- extended training benefits up to 2½ years to allow for remedial training for those who need it;
- extended income support to match the allowable training period, including up to 2 years after workers exhaust their regular Unemployment Insurance (UI) benefits;
- doubled the amount of funds available for training to $220 million per year;
- established a deadline for workers to enroll in training, after they have been laid off or their petition has been approved, in order to maintain eligibility for extended income support payments;
- created a wage insurance benefit for workers age 50 and older, subsidizing the difference between the prior and new wages of some trade-affected workers who find reemployment quickly;
- created a health coverage tax credit to help trade-affected workers pay for health insurance; and

- shortened from 60 days to 40 days the time the Labor is given to process petitions filed on behalf of groups of workers to determine their potential eligibility for services.

You asked us to provide an overview of the TAA program as it currently operates. This testimony provides information on (1) how the program operates, (2) recent trends in Labor's certification of petitions, (3) the extent to which workers' participate in training, (4) the extent to which workers take advantage of other TAA benefits, and (5) what is known about TAA program outcomes. To address these issues, we drew upon our recently issued report prepared for you, as well as on our prior study of five trade-related layoffs and our review of TAA performance data. Our most recent study was based, in part, on a survey of the 46 states that received an initial allocation of TAA training funds in federal fiscal year 2006 (October 1, 2005, to September 30, 2006).[2] We received responses from all 46 states. In addition, we interviewed Labor officials and visited state and local officials in four states—California, Massachusetts, Michigan, and North Carolina. The case study review examined in detail five plant closures located in Massachusetts, Mississippi, Missouri, Pennsylvania, and Washington that were certified under TAA.[3] We visited each layoff site and interviewed state and local officials, company and union officials, training providers, and affected workers. In addition, we conducted a telephone survey of all affected workers, including those who did not receive services. Survey response rates for each layoff ranged from 66 percent to 86 percent. In conducting the TAA performance data review, we conducted a survey of the 46 states that received an initial allocation of TAA training funds in federal fiscal year 2005, and obtained a 100 percent response rate. In addition, we visited five states—California, Iowa, Ohio, Texas, and Virginia—and interviewed state and local officials. We performed our work in accordance with generally accepted government auditing standards.

In summary, TAA provides a variety of benefits and services to workers who lose their jobs because of international trade, including income support, job training, and health coverage. Workers typically access these services through one-stop centers where they also receive case management services, such as counseling and vocational assessments. Our work shows that during the past 3 fiscal years, there has been a decline in the number of petitions filed and certified. However, the proportion of petitions Labor has certified over the 3 years remained relatively stable at about two-thirds and covered an estimated 400,000 workers. Nationally, the decline in the number of workers entering training from fiscal years 2004 to 2006 parallels a decline in the estimated number of trade-affected workers—declining sharply between fiscal years 2004 to 2005 but leveling off in fiscal year 2006. However, trends in the number of workers entering training vary from state to state. Not all workers choose to enroll in training. In our study of five layoffs, no more than 40 percent of affected workers at any site enrolled in training, and at one site, only 9 percent enrolled. Occupational training remains the most popular type of training, currently constituting about three-quarters of all training enrollments. We also found that few TAA participants take advantage of the wage insurance and health coverage benefits. Although the number of new workers receiving the wage insurance benefit has increased from 1,400 in 2004 to about 3,200 in 2006, the number remains small—two-thirds of the states estimate that 5 percent or less of their TAA participants received wage insurance in fiscal year 2006. Participation in the health coverage benefit is also low. Approximately 6,900 workers enrolled for the first time in the advanced health coverage benefit in fiscal year 2006. Finally, we found that the nationwide TAA performance data that are currently available do not provide a complete and credible picture of the program's performance. However, at our five case study sites, we found that most of the workers who lost their jobs because of foreign trade had either found a job or retired at the time of our survey. The majority of reemployed workers earned less in their new jobs than they had previously earned, but according to our survey estimates generally replaced about 80 percent or more of their prelayoff wages.

An Overview of the TAA Process from Filing Petitions to Receiving Benefits

The process for enrolling trade-affected workers in the TAA program begins when a petition for TAA assistance is filed with Labor on behalf of a group of workers. Once certified, workers may receive a variety of benefits, including income support, job training, and health coverage. Workers typically access these services through the one-stop system—the consolidated service delivery system required under the Workforce Investment Act (WIA) to provide services for most federally funded employment and training programs. Case managers at the one-stop centers also provide vocational assessments and counseling to help workers enroll in the program and decide which services or benefits are most appropriate.

TAA Petition Process

Petitions may be filed by the employer experiencing the layoff, a group of at least three affected workers, a union, or the state or local workforce agency. Labor is required to either certify or deny the petition within 40 days after receiving it. Labor investigates whether a petition meets the requirements for TAA certification by taking steps such as contacting company officials, surveying a company's customers, and examining aggregate industry data. When Labor has certified a petition, it notifies the relevant state, which has responsibility for contacting the workers covered by the petition, informing them of the benefits available to them, and telling them when and where to apply for benefits. The TAA statute lays out certain basic requirements that all certified petitions must meet, including that a significant proportion of workers employed by a company be laid off or threatened with layoff and that affected workers must have been employed by a company that produces articles.[4] In addition to meeting these basic requirements, a petition must demonstrate that the layoff is related to international trade in one of several ways, including the following:

- Increased imports—imports of articles that are similar to or directly compete with articles produced by the firm have increased, the sales or production of the firm has decreased, and the increase in imports has contributed importantly to the decline in sales or production and the layoff or threatened layoff of workers.
- Shift of production—the firm has shifted production of articles to another country and either
    - the country is party to a free trade agreement with the United States or
    - the country is a beneficiary under the Andean Trade Preference Act, the African Growth and Opportunity Act, or the Caribbean Basin Economic Recovery Act or
    - there has been or is likely to be an increase in imports of articles that are similar to or directly compete with articles produced by the firm.
- Affected secondarily by trade—workers must meet one of two criteria:
    - Upstream secondary workers—affected firm produces and supplies component parts to another firm that has experienced TAA-certified layoffs, parts supplied to the certified firm

constituted at least 20 percent of the affected firm's production, or a loss of business with the certified firm contributed importantly to the layoffs at the affected firm.

- Downstream secondary workers—affected firm performs final assembly or finishing work for another firm that has experienced TAA-certified layoffs as a result of an increase in imports from or a shift in production to Canada or Mexico, and a loss of business with the certified firm contributed importantly to the layoffs at the affected firm.

If Labor denies a petition for TAA assistance, the workers who would have been certified under the petition have two options for challenging this denial. They may request an administrative reconsideration of the decision by Labor. To take this step, workers must provide reasons why the denial is erroneous based on either a mistake or misinterpretation of the facts or the law itself, and must mail their request to Labor within 30 days of the announcement of the denial. Workers may also appeal to the United States Court of International Trade for judicial review of Labor's denial within 60 days of either the initial denial or a denial following administrative reconsideration by Labor.

State and local workforce agencies also play key roles in the petition certification process and help workers take advantage of the services and benefits available in TAA. The agencies assist workers and employers in filing petitions and will also file petitions on behalf of workers. After a petition is certified, the agencies contact employers to obtain a list of workers affected by the layoff and send each worker a letter notifying him or her of potential eligibility. The agencies may also hold orientation sessions to provide workers with detailed information on the TAA program and services and benefits that workers typically access through the one-stop system. Case managers at the one-stop centers provide vocational assessments and counseling to help workers enroll in the program and decide which services or benefits are most appropriate. Local case managers also refer workers to other programs, such as the Workforce Investment Act, for additional services.

TAA Benefits and Services

Under TAA, workers enrolled in the program have access to a variety of benefits and services including the following:

Training

Participants may receive up to 130 weeks of training, including 104 weeks of vocational training and 26 weeks of remedial training, such as English as a second language.

Extended income support

Participants may receive a total of 104 weeks of extended income support beyond the 26 weeks of unemployment insurance (UI) benefits available in most states. In fiscal year 2006, Congress appropriated about $655 million for income support.

Job search and relocation benefits

Payments are available to help participants search for a job in a different geographical area and to relocate to a different area to take a job. Labor distributed a total of about $288, 000 in fiscal year 2006 for these benefits.

Wage insurance benefit

The wage insurance benefit, known as the Alternative Trade Adjustment Assistance (ATAA) program, was created by the TAA Reform Act of 2002 as a demonstration project for workers age 50 years old or older and who find reemployment within 26 weeks of being laid off that pays less than $50,000 and less than what they previously earned. Workers who meet these criteria are eligible to receive 50 percent of the difference between their new and old wages up to a maximum of $10,000 over 2 years. For the fiscal year 2008 budget request, Labor estimated wage insurance benefits at $23 million.

Health coverage benefit

The health coverage benefit, known as the Health Coverage Tax Credit (HCTC) and also created by the TAA Reform Act, helps workers pay for health care insurance through a tax credit.[5] Workers can choose to receive the benefit in one of two ways—as an advance option that covers 65 percent of their monthly premiums, allowing them to lower the amount they have to pay out of pocket for health coverage, or as an end-of-year tax credit that is claimed on their income taxes. To be eligible for the health coverage benefit, workers must either be (1) receiving extended income support payments, or eligible for extended income support but still receiving UI payments, or (2) receiving the wage insurance benefit. IRS administers the health coverage tax credit program. There are three health plan options that are automatically eligible:

- *COBRA continuation plans.* Under the Consolidated Omnibus Budget Reconciliation Act (COBRA) of 1985, certain employers with 20 or more employees are required to make available 18 to 36 months of continued health care coverage for former employees and their dependents who lose health coverage due to certain circumstances, such as when a worker is laid off.
- *Spousal coverage.* Health care insurance obtained through the employer of a worker's spouse is also eligible, provided that the employer contributed less than 50 percent toward the cost of coverage.
- *Individual market plans.* Workers may use the health coverage benefit to cover a portion of the monthly cost of individually purchased health coverage if the worker purchased the coverage at least 30 days prior to being laid off.

In addition to the three options that are automatically qualified for the health coverage benefit, the TAA Reform Act allows states to designate other coverage alternatives—called state-qualified options. These state- qualified plans must, among other requirements, provide coverage for preexisting conditions. Currently, 43 have state-qualified plans.

Certifications Have Declined over Past 3 Fiscal Years as Petition Filings Declined

During the past 3 fiscal years, the number of petitions certified and the number of petitions filed have declined. The proportion of petitions certified has remained relatively stable, as Labor certified about two-thirds of petitions investigated in each of these years. These petitions covered an estimated 400,000 workers. Petitions were most commonly denied because workers were not involved in the production of articles, a basic requirement of the TAA program.

Labor Certified Two-Thirds of Petitions Investigated, although the Number of Certifications Declined as Petitions Filed Declined

Over the past 3 fiscal years, the number of petitions certified has declined 17 percent, from nearly 1,700 in fiscal year 2004 to 1,400 in fiscal year 2006. Labor certified two-thirds of petitions that it investigated over the past 3 fiscal years, certifying nearly 4,700 petitions (see table 1).

An estimated 400,000 workers were covered by petitions between fiscal years 2004 and 2006. However, because layoffs tend to be episodic, the estimated number of trade-affected workers fluctuates dramatically from year to year and state to state. For example, the estimated number of trade-affected workers being laid off declined dramatically in Kansas from fiscal years 2004 to 2005—from 4,117 in 2004 to 75 workers in 2005— and increased somewhat in 2006 to 721. Overall the estimated number of trade- affected workers in Kansas laid off in fiscal year 2006 represented about an 80 percent decrease from the estimated number in 2004. On the other hand, Missouri experienced an 80 percent increase in the number of trade-affected workers being laid off between fiscal years 2004 and 2006—from 1,275 to 2,301 (see figure 1).

Table 1. TAA Petition Filings and Investigation Decisions, Fiscal Years 2004 to 2006.

Fiscal year	Number of petitions filed	Number investigated[a]	Number certified	Number denied	Percentage certified
2004	2,992	2,559	1,689	870	66
2005	2,638	2,358	1,589	769	67
2006	2,456	2,232	1,407	825	63
Total past 3 years	8,086	7,149	4,685[b]	2,464[c]	66

Source: GAO analysis of Department of Labor petitions data.

[a] About 900 petitions were terminated prior to an investigation by the Department of Labor during fiscal years 2004 to 2006, accounting for 12 percent of petitions filed. Petitions may be terminated for several reasons, including that a petition was recently denied for the layoff or a company official was not available to provide necessary information.

[b] The numbers on petitions certified include 12 petitions that were partially certified.

[c] Labor initially denied 2,599 petitions, but 135 were reversed upon appeal.

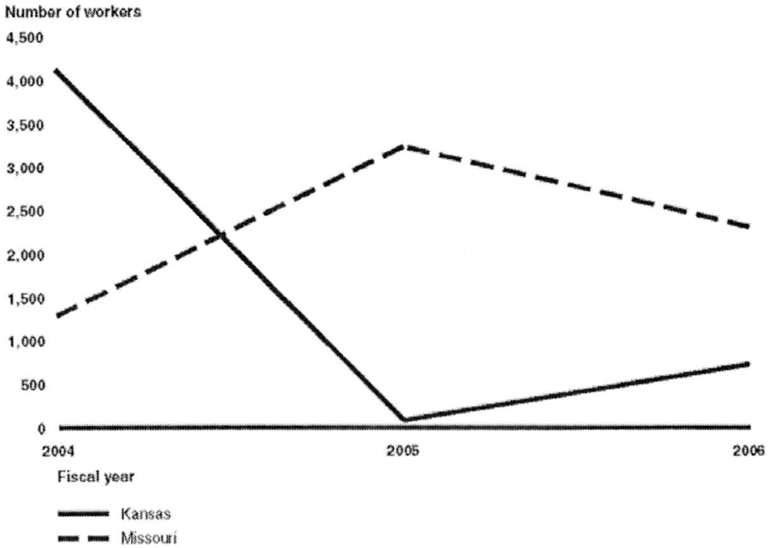

Source: GAO analysis of Department of Labor petitions data.

Figure 1. Fluctuation in Estimated Number of Trade-Affected Workers Laid Off from Fiscal Years 2004 to 2006 in Kansas and Missouri.

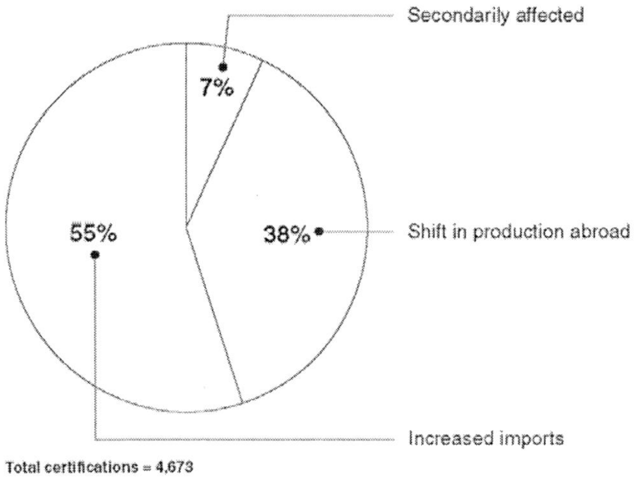

Source: GAO analysis of Department of Labor data on petitions filed during fiscal years 2004 to 2006.

Note: This figure does not include 12 petitions that were partially certified.

Figure 2. Categories under Which TAA Petitions Were Certified, Fiscal Years 2004-2006.

Of the approximately 4,700 petitions certified over the past 3 fiscal years, most qualified for the TAA program because increased imports contributed to the layoff of workers. An additional 38 percent of certified petitions were because workers lost jobs due to a shift in production to another country (see figure 2).

Although petitions for secondarily affected workers constitute only 7 percent of certified petitions, the number of workers covered under this eligibility requirement has increased somewhat, from about 7,900 workers in fiscal year 2004 to 8,800 workers in fiscal year 2006.[6] Nearly all of the 328 petitions certified for secondarily affected workers during the past 3 fiscal years were for workers at firms that supplied component parts to another firm that experienced a TAA-certified layoff, or upstream firms.

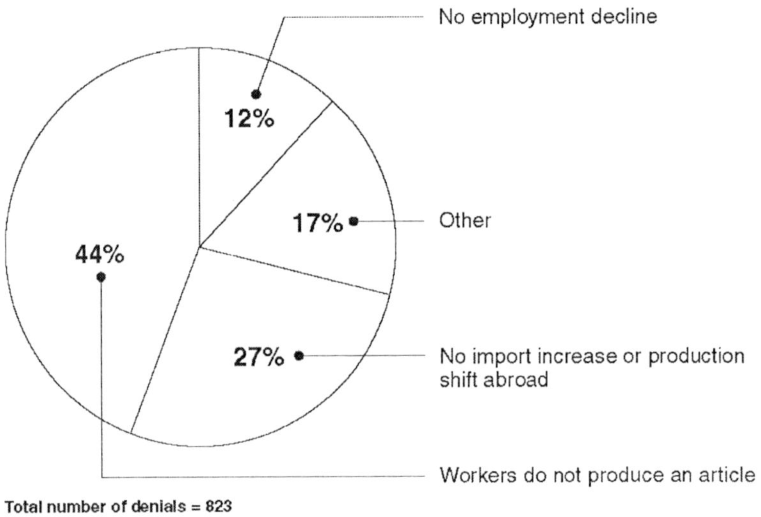

Source: GAO analysis of Department of Labor data on petitions filed during fiscal year 2006.

Note: Other reasons that petitions were denied were that the company did not experience a decline in sales or production, the predominant cause of the layoff was unrelated to imports or a shift in production abroad, or there was no secondary impact. This figure does not include two petitions that were missing information on reasons they were denied.

Figure 3. Reasons Petitions Filed in Fiscal Year 2006 Were Denied.

Labor has generally processed petitions in a timely manner over the past 3 fiscal years. Labor's average processing time has remained relatively steady, taking on average 32 days to conduct an investigation and determine whether to certify or deny the petition. Labor met the requirement to process petitions within 40 days for 77 percent of petitions it investigated during fiscal years 2004 to 2006. Labor most often took only an extra day to process the remaining petitions. Labor officials said that the reason they are not always able to meet the 40-day time frame is because they sometimes do not receive necessary information in a timely manner from company officials.

Petitions Were Most Often Denied because Workers Were Not Involved in Producing an Article

During the past 3 fiscal years, about 2,500 petitions have been denied, and in fiscal year 2006, the most common reason for petitions being denied was because workers were not involved in producing an article, a basic requirement of the TAA program.[7] Of the over 800 petitions filed in fiscal year 2006 that were denied, 359 (44 percent) were denied for this reason (see figure 3).

Of the 359 petitions denied because workers did not produce articles, about one-third were for business services, such as computer programming, and about one-third were for airport-related services, such as aircraft maintenance. During the past 3 fiscal years, workers appealed decisions in 16 percent of the approximately 2,600 petitions that Labor initially denied. The vast majority were appealed directly to Labor. Labor's decisions were reversed in one-third of the appeals. Labor officials told us that appeals are often reversed because Labor receives new information, as part of the appeals process, that justifies certifying the petition. Although few denied petitions are appealed to the U.S. Court of International Trade (CIT), many of the recent appeals concern the issue of whether workers were involved in the production of articles.

NUMBER OF WORKERS ENROLLING IN TRAINING HAS DECLINED SINCE 2003

Nationally, the decline in the number of workers entering training from 2004 to 2006 parallels the decline in the estimated number of workers covered under certifications during this period (see figure 4). However, there are wide state-to-state variations in this trend. Sixteen states responding to our recent survey reported a decrease in training enrollment during the past 3 fiscal years, while 20 states reported an increase. States reporting a decline said that the state experienced fewer layoffs, had fewer eligible participants, and many workers needed to go back to work, rather than enter training. States reporting increases had experienced several large plant closures, had larger percentages of workers needing remedial training, and had more employers that required their workers to have higher skill levels.

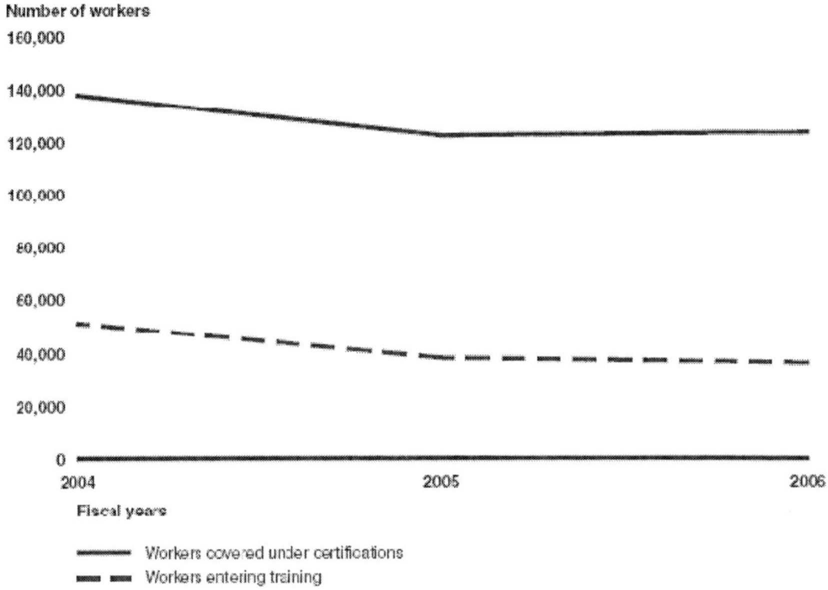

Source: GAO analysis of Department of Labor petitions dataand quarterly activity reports.

Figure 4. Number of TAA Participants Covered under Certifications and Enrolled in Training by Fiscal Year.

While many affected workers may seek employment services at one-stop centers, relatively few enroll in training, according to the results of our study of five layoffs. Seventy-percent or more of the workers in our study visited a one-stop center, often receiving one-on-one assistance. In our most recent study, we found that, nationally, occupational training remains the largest training category for TAA participants, with about three-fourths of TAA training participants opting for occupational training. States ranked nursing—including registered nurses, licensed practical nurses, and certified vocational nurses—medical assisting, and truck driving as the occupations in which TAA participants were most frequently trained. Although occupational training remains the largest training category, its relative percentage has decreased, while the percentage of training enrollments for remedial education has increased (see table 2).[8]

For our most recent study, some local officials told us that the need for remedial training had increased, in part because more non-English- speaking workers were being laid off. For example, officials from local areas in two states we visited said that most workers who opted for training enrolled in English as a second language (ESL) courses. In response to this need, training providers in one of the local areas designed a specific training program for dislocated garment workers that enabled workers to take both ESL and occupational skills training simultaneously.

Table 2. Training Enrollments by Type of Training by Fiscal Year.

Type of Training	2004		2005		2006	
	Number	Percent	Number	Percent	Number	Percent
Occupational	42,793	84	29,909	79	27,101	75
Remedial	7,768	15	7,509	20	8,239	23
On-the-job	368	1	356	1	590	2
Total	**50,929**	**100**	**37, 774**	**100**	**35,930**	**100**

Source: Department of Labor data.

Note: On-the-job training (OJT) is training provided by an employer in the public or private sector to a TAA participant that has been hired by the employer. Under the OJT contract, the employer is reimbursed for no more than 50 percent of the participant's wage for a specified duration.

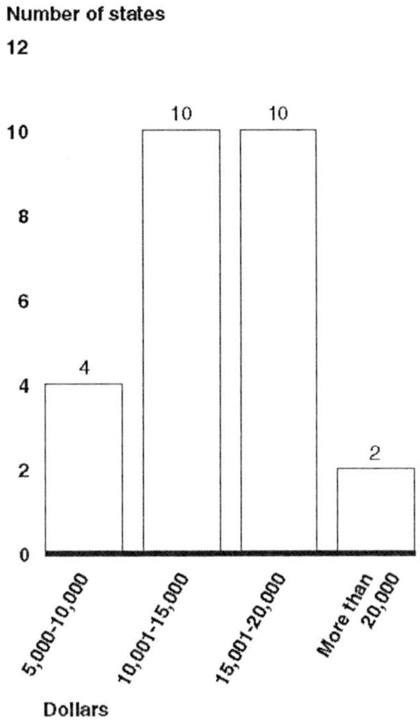

Source: GAO analysis of survey responses.

Figure 5. States' Training Cost Limits.

Twenty six of the 46 states we surveyed reported having a maximum amount they will pay for a worker to attend training, typically from $10,000 to $20,000 (see figure 5). Many of these states did, however, note that their training maximums were flexible and could be waived if justified. In addition, 13 states in our survey reported that their training cost limits had increased during the past 3 years, mainly due to rises in tuition and related expenses, as well as requests for more expensive training.

Most workers who entered training at the five case study sites enrolled in programs that were relatively short-term and that cost less than $10,000. At four sites, half or more of the workers who enrolled in training were enrolled in programs expected to last 1 year or less, and at three of these sites, about 30 percent or more of the workers in training entered programs expected to last 6 months or less(see figure 6).

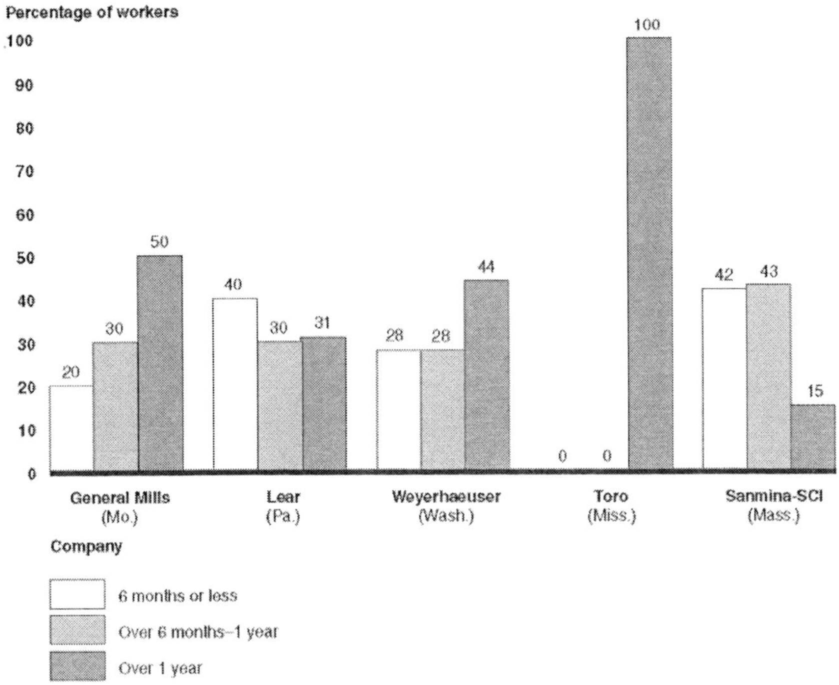

Source: State administrative records.

Notes: Data on training duration were available for 105 General Mills workers, 91 Lear workers, 25 Weyerhaeuser workers, 7 Toro workers, and 139 Sanmina-SCI workers. Because of rounding, totals do not always equal 100 percent.

Figure 6. Workers in TAA- or WIA-Funded Training, by Expected Length of Training Program.

At our five case study sites we found that while most workers at each site had received income support benefits, up to one-third received no income support at all. Only about a third or less of the workers at each site had received the benefits for over 1 year, and no more than 8 percent for longer than 18 months. Because most workers in the sites we studied did not enroll in training, and those who did most commonly entered programs lasting 1 year or less, the vast majority of the workers in these sites did not utilize the full 2 years of extended income support benefits available to them (see figure 7).

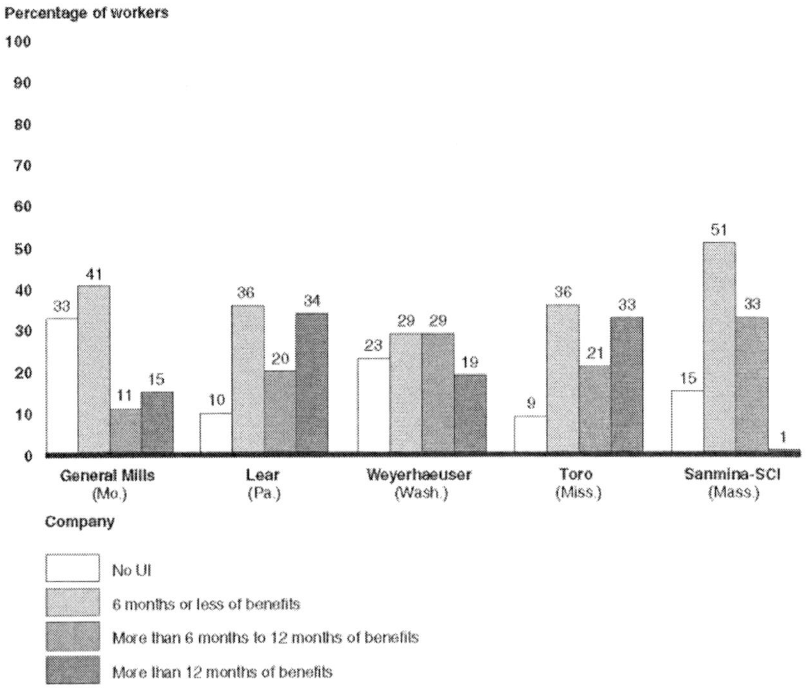

Source: GAO survey of dislocated workers.

Notes: Data include workers still receiving UI or extended income support benefits at the time of our survey. For example, the Sanmina-SCI plant closure occurred about 8 months before our survey, and 49 percent of Sanmina-SCI workers were still receiving income support benefits at the time of our survey. Because of rounding, totals do not always equal 100 percent.

Figure 7. Number of Months Workers Received Income Support Benefits (UI and in Some Cases Extended Income Support).

FEW TAA PARTICIPANTS TAKE ADVANTAGE OF WAGE INSURANCE AND HEALTH COVERAGE BENEFITS

While participation remains low, the number of workers entering the wage insurance program has increased from 2004 to 2006—from about 1,400 in 2004 to about 3,200 in 2006 (see figure 8).

The universe of workers eligible for wage insurance cannot be estimated because data are not available on the number of workers certified for TAA who are 50 years old or older and meet the other eligibility requirements.

However, two-thirds of the states we surveyed estimated that 5 percent or less of TAA participants received wage insurance in fiscal year 2006. In our study of five layoffs, we found that no more than one in five of the workers potentially eligible for the wage insurance benefit received it. In 2006, wage insurance benefits totaling $16.7 million were paid to about 6,300 workers. The total yearly benefits remain far lower than the 2002 Congressional Budget Office estimate of $50 million per year.

Participation levels remain low for the health coverage benefit. Although the number of TAA participants enrolling for the first time in the advance health coverage benefit—whereby participants receive a monthly tax credit that covers 65 percent of their premiums—has increased since 2004, only about 6,900 received the advance health benefit for the first time in fiscal year 2006. TAA participants may also elect to receive an end-of-year tax credit, but the number of TAA participants selecting this option is also low and has been decreasing over time. We estimate that for tax year 2005, approximately 5,700 TAA participants received end-of-year tax credits.

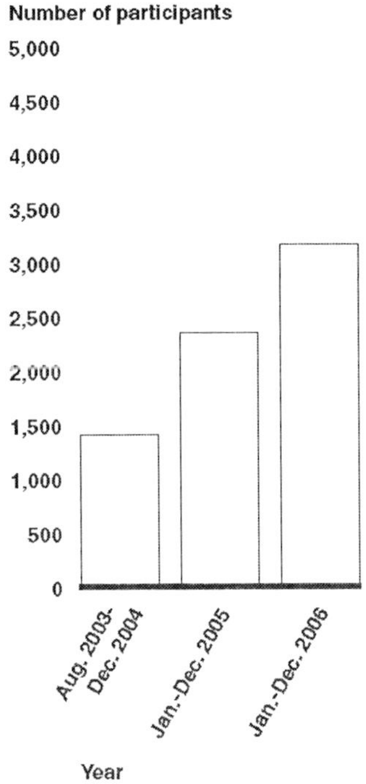

Source: Department of Labor data.

Figure 8. Wage Insurance Enrollments, Calendar Years 2004 to 2006.

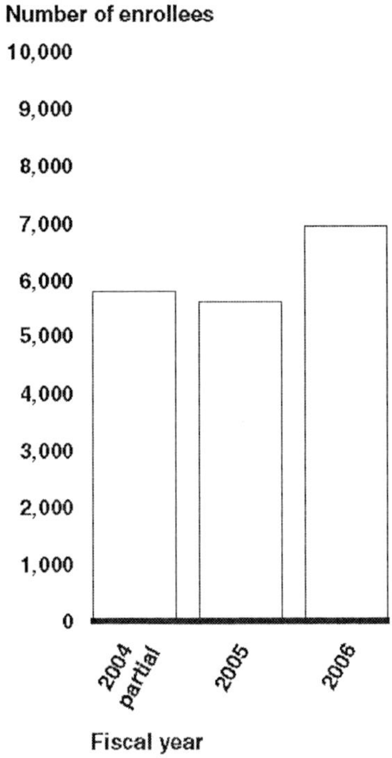

Source: GAO analysis of IRS data.

Notes: IRS data on new advance credit enrollments are unavailable prior to January 2004.

Figure 9. Advance Health Coverage Benefit Enrollments, Fiscal Years 2004 to 2006.

New enrollments in the advance credit option have increased over the past 2 fiscal years, from about 5,600 to about 6,900 enrollments (see figure 9). As of September 2006, approximately 7 percent of the workers that were eligible for the extended income support, a basic requirement for the health coverage benefit, were receiving the advance credit. However, some of the workers that were eligible for extended income support may not meet other eligibility requirements for the health coverage benefit, such as having a qualified health plan. Since inception of the advance benefit, about 22,000 TAA participants have received the credit.

Little Is Known Nationwide about What the Program Achieves

The TAA programwide performance data that are currently available do not provide a complete and credible picture of the program's performance. In our 2006 review of TAA performance data, we found that the data that Labor uses to calculate program outcomes, such as reemployment and retention rates, did not include all participants who had completed the program. Only half the states reported that the data they submit to Labor for determining progress toward national performance goals include all TAA participants who stop receiving benefits or services—that is, exit the TAA program, as Labor requires. We found that Labor did not have a process in place to ensure that states included all exiting participants in their data. As a result, the performance data are incomplete and may be skewed. In addition, some states were not using all available data sources to determine TAA participants' employment outcomes. This may result in lower reported outcomes because states may be inaccurately recording some workers as unemployed who actually have jobs. To compile TAA data, some states have information technology (IT) systems with limited capabilities that may hinder their ability to ensure that the TAA data are complete and accurate. Nine states were using manual rather than automated processes to compile their TAA performance data, increasing the data's vulnerability to data entry errors, and only about half of the states' TAA IT systems could perform edit checks to help minimize errors. State officials said resource shortages contributed to their data problems, but many states planned to make improvements to their TAA IT systems' capabilities. At the end of fiscal year 2006, Labor distributed $250,000 to each state to help them improve their TAA performance data systems, but it is too soon to know whether their efforts will improve the quality of the data.

Because nationwide outcome data are limited, our study of five layoffs examined the outcomes for workers affected by these layoffs. We found that most of the workers who lost their jobs because of foreign trade at four of the five sites we studied had either found a job or retired at the time of our survey (see figure 10).

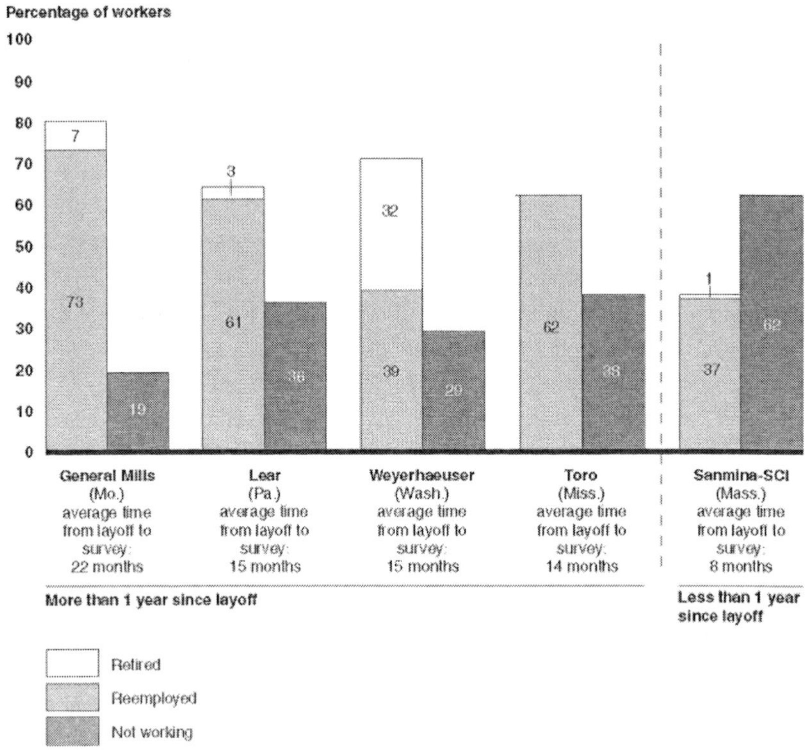

Source: GAO survey of dislocated workers.

Figure 10. Most Workers at Four of Five Sites Had Found Jobs or Retired at the Time of the Survey.

The workers who had entered training were the least likely to be reemployed at each site, but it may be too soon to know the effect of training on employment outcomes. Some of the workers who had enrolled in training were expected to still be in training at the time of our survey. Workers who did not go to a one-stop center were at least as likely to be reemployed as those who visited a one-stop (but did not get training). At only two sites—Weyerhaeuser and Sanmina-SCI—were workers who did not visit a one-stop center more likely to be reemployed than those who did. For example, at Weyerhaeuser, 50 percent of those who did not visit a one-stop center were reemployed, compared with 39 percent of those who did visit a one-stop center but did not get training.

Table 3. Average Prelayoff Hourly Wage and Wage Replacement Rates.

Company	Went to one-stop and enrolled in training		Went to one-stop but did not enroll in training		Did not go to one-stop	
	Average pre-layoff hourly wage (in dollars)	Average wage replacement rate when reemployed (percent)	Average pre-layoff hourly wage (in dollars)	Average wage replacement rate when reemployed (percent)	Average pre-layoff hourly wage (in dollars)	Average wage replacement rate when reemployed (percent)
General Mills	$15.67	82	$16.49	88	$17.97	95
Lear	16.22	92[a]	16.13	74	17.26	94
Weyerhaeuser	25.35	71[a]	27.10	87	30.34	93[c]
Toro	13.83	[b]	15.21	81	[b]	[b]
Sanmina-SCI	16.79	89	18.46	94	22.96	96[c]

Source: GAO survey of dislocated workers.

Notes: Some of the workers who entered training—ranging from about one-third to over 60 percent among the 5 sites—were expected to still be in training at the time of our survey, and it may have been more difficult for these workers to have started a new job. Differences between estimates of average wage replacement rates for workers who did not visit a one-stop center versus those who did were not statistically significant at the 95 percent confidence interval at Weyerhaeuser and Sanmina-SCI.

[a] These estimates have margins of error of plus or minus 15 percent or less of the value of the estimates.

[b] All Toro workers went to a one-stop center. None of the Toro workers who went to training have become employed, according to administrative data. However, all but one were expected to still be in training at the time of our survey.

The majority of reemployed workers earned less in their new jobs than they had previously earned, but according to our survey estimates generally replaced about 80 percent or more of their prelayoff wages. Workers and officials told us that several of the plants that we studied paid higher wages than other companies in the area. Unless workers moved out of the area, they could not easily earn comparable wages doing the same type of work.

Workers at four of the five sites who did not go to a one-stop center had a higher average prelayoff wage than those who did. For example, Weyerhaeuser workers who did not go to a one-stop center had an average prelayoff wage of about $30 an hour, while those who visited a one-stop center (but did not get training) had an average pre-layoff wage of about $27 an hour. When reemployed, workers who did not visit a one-stop center generally replaced at least the same proportion of their prelayoff wages as those who did.[9] With the exception of employees at Lear, those who received training had the lowest average prelayoff wages. And at two of five sites, these workers had the lowest average wage replacement rate when reemployed (see table 3).

More than half of reemployed workers returned to the manufacturing sector, and at most sites workers who returned to manufacturing replaced about the same proportion of their prelayoff wages as workers who entered other fields. Workers who entered training replaced slightly less of their wages than workers who did not at all but one site, and those who were trained generally left manufacturing for another industry. When reemployed workers did not return to manufacturing, we found they entered fields such as professional and business services; trade, transportation, and utilities; construction; and education, health care, and social services. To determine whether participant outcomes are a result of services, rather than other factors, it is necessary to conduct an impact evaluation that can take these and other factors into account. Labor has funded a long-term study to assess the impact of TAA program services. Data collection began in 2005 and will continue until 2008, and a final report is scheduled to be issued by the end of 2008.

Concluding Observations

The TAA program targets manufacturing workers affected by international trade, who may have fewer transferable skills and face greater challenges to reemployment than other dislocated workers. The program provides a unique blend of services and benefits that have been designed to meet these workers' needs—some of which are not available to other dislocated workers. But little has been known about whether the services provided are the right mix for today's workers who are dislocated due to trade. Our case study provided a glimpse of the needs of a small group of workers, the services they received, and their employment outcomes about 8 to 22 months after their layoffs.

Workers affected by layoffs take a variety of paths. Workers are increasingly taking advantage of wage insurance and health coverage benefits, but the numbers remain fairly small. In our case study, we learned that a large majority sought some assistance from their one-stop center. Relatively few chose to enroll in training, but those who did often used this opportunity to chart a new career path. A few did not seek any federally funded reemployment services, and yet were still successful in getting a new job. We cannot know all the factors that motivate workers to seek particular services or that affect their employability, and we cannot assess the role that TAA services played in the outcomes workers achieved. It may be that some workers make an independent assessment of what they need to help them rejoin the workforce and then try to take the necessary steps, such as seeking services at a one-stop, to make that happen.

End Notes

[1] For further information on TAA, please see the following reports: GAO, *Trade Adjustment Assistance: Changes to Funding Allocation and Eligibility Requirements Could Enhance States' Ability to Provide Benefits and Services*. GAO-07-701, GAO-07-702. (Washington, D.C.: May XX, 2007; *Trade Adjustment Assistance: Labor Should Take Action to Ensure Performance Data Are Complete, Accurate, and Accessible*. GAO-06-496. (Washington, D.C.: Apr. 25, 2006); *Trade Adjustment Assistance: Most Workers in Five Layoffs Received Services, but Better Outreach Needed on New Benefits*. GAO-06-43. (Washington, D.C.: Jan. 31, 2006); and *Trade Adjustment Assistance: Reforms Have Accelerated Training Enrollment, but Implementation Challenges Remain*. GAO-04-1012. (Washington, D.C.: Sept. 22, 2004).

[2] The four states that did not receive an initial allocation of TAA training funds in fiscal year 2006 were Delaware, Hawaii, North Dakota, and Wyoming.

[3] The selected plant closures were: Massachusetts, Sanmina-SCI Corporation (printed circuit boards); Mississippi, the Toro Company (lawnmower and snow-thrower engines); Missouri, General Mills, Inc. (baked goods); Pennsylvania, Lear Corporation (automotive carpets); and Washington, Weyerhaeuser Company (fine paper and pulp).

[4] The statute provides that Labor determine that a significant number or portion of workers have become totally or partially separated, or are threatened to become totally or partially separated. 19 U.S.C. § 2272(a)(1).

[5] The Trade Adjustment Assistance Reform Act of 2002 created a health coverage tax credit for certain workers who are eligible to receive income support benefits under the TAA program because their jobs were lost due to foreign competition and for certain retirees whose

pensions from a former employer were terminated and are now paid by the Pension Benefit Guaranty Corporation (PBGC).

[6] The data used to estimate the number of workers certified as eligible for TAA are based on estimates of the number of affected workers submitted by companies at the time TAA petitions are filed with the Department of Labor. At the time petitions are submitted, companies may not know exactly how many workers will be affected.

[7] Fiscal year 2006 was the first year that complete data were available on the reasons petitions were denied.

[8] The percentages are based on enrollments in each training category and not individuals. Some individuals could have enrolled in more than one activity.

[9] At the fifth site, Toro, in Mississippi, all workers went to a one-stop center. Therefore, we could not compare the employment outcomes for those who visited a center to the outcomes for those who did not.

In: Global Competition
Editors: Dianna J. Hall et al.
ISBN: 978-1-61324-712-9

Chapter 6

TRADE ADJUSTMENT ASSISTANCE FOR COMMUNITIES: THE LAW AND ITS IMPLEMENTATION

Eugene Boyd

SUMMARY

On August 18, 2009, the Department of Commerce's Economic Development Administration (EDA) published in the *Federal Register* final rules and regulations governing Trade Adjustment Assistance for Communities (TAAC) program. The regulations outline the responsibilities of EDA in administering the program, including determining a community's eligibility for TAAC grants, providing technical assistance to impacted communities, and evaluating grant applications. On January 11, 2010, EDA published in the *Federal Register* a notice soliciting applications for TAAC grants. Concurrently, it published the full announcement and application for assistance at http://www.grants.gov and established April 20, 2010, as the deadline for applications.

The TAAC grant program was created with the passage of the American Recovery and Reinvestment Act (ARRA) of 2009, P.L. 111-5. Included among the subtitles of Division B of ARRA, was the Trade and Globalization Adjustment Assistance Act (TGAAA) of 2009. The TAAC program, as authorized by ARRA, comprises four subchapters:

- Subchapter A—Trade Adjustment Assistance to Communities (TAAC) directs the EDA to provide technical assistance and to award strategic planning and implementation grants to eligible trade-impacted communities.
- Subchapter B—Community Colleges and Career Training (CC&CT) creates a competitive grant program administered by the Department of Labor which is intended to strengthen the role of community colleges in filling the education and skills gap of workers in trade impacted communities.
- Subchapter C—Industry or Sector Partnership Grants Program for Communities Impacted by Trade (ISG) creates a grant program intended to encourage the creation of public private partnerships that develop a skilled workforce.
- Subchapter D—General Provisions includes language prohibiting workers receiving trade adjustment assistance from being disqualified from receiving assistance under activities funded by the TAAC program.

The Supplemental Appropriations Act of 2009, P.L. 111-32, included a $40 million appropriation that funded both TAAC and Trade Adjustment Assistance for Firms. For FY2010, the Consolidated Appropriations Act for FY2010, P.L. 111-117, included an appropriation of $15.8 million to be shared between the trade adjustment assistance programs for communities and firms. In addition, on March 30, 2010, the President signed the Health Care and Education Reconciliation Act of 2010, P.L. 111-152, which included $500 million in funding for each of the fiscal years FY2011 through FY2014 for Subchapter B, Community Colleges and Career Training Grants.

Recent Developments

On August 18, 2009, the Department of Commerce's Economic Development Administration (EDA) published in the *Federal Register* final rules and regulations governing the implementation of the Trade Adjustment Assistance for Communities (TAAC) grant program. The regulations outline the responsibilities of EDA in administering the program including determining a community's eligibility for TAAC planning and implementation grants, providing technical assistance to impacted communities, and evaluating grant applications. On January 11, 2010, EDA published in the *Federal*

Register a notice soliciting applications for TAAC grant assistance. The notice set April 20, 2010, as the deadline for the submission of applications for TAAC grants, established the criteria for awarding funds and directed potential applicants to the grants.gov website for the complete application.[1]

Overview of the Trade Adjustment Assistance for Communities (TAAC) Program

The TAAC grant program was created with the passage of the American Recovery and Reinvestment Act (ARRA) of 2009, P.L. 111-5, as part of a larger effort by the Obama Administration and the 111th Congress to address an economic recession that began in December 2007.[2] Included among the subtitles of Division B of ARRA was the Trade and Globalization Adjustment Assistance Act (TGAAA) of 2009.[3] TGAAA amends the Trade Act of 1974,[4] extending and revising trade adjustment assistance provisions affecting various constituencies including trade-impacted workers, farmers, firms, and communities.[5] Included among the amendments to the Trade Act were provisions reestablishing a Trade Adjustment Assistance for Communities (TAAC) grant program.[6]

The TAAC program, as authorized by ARRA, comprises of four subchapters:

- Subchapter A establishes the TAAC programs within the Department of Commerce;
- Subchapter B creates the Community College and Career Training Grant program;
- Subchapter C establishes Industry or Sector Partnership Grants program for Communities Impacted by Trade; and
- Subchapter D includes general provisions related to program implementation.

Subchapter A—Trade Adjustment Assistance for Communities (TAAC)

The 2009 amendments to Chapter 4 of Title II of the Trade Act of 1974 directed the Department of Commerce (DOC) to establish a trade adjustment assistance program for communities by August 1, 2009. The act identified key components and processes of the TAAC program, including provisions governing the responsibilities of the DOC, eligible program activities, and cost sharing and reporting requirements.

Within the DOC, the Economic Development Administration (EDA) was designated the agency responsible for administering the new TAAC grant program. EDA is charged with:

- making *affirmative determination* of a community's eligibility for assistance;
- providing technical assistance to eligible communities;
- awarding strategic planning and project implementation grants to eligible communities; and
- establishing an Interagency Community Assistance Working Group responsible for coordinating federal assistance to trade-impacted communities.

Notifying Communities of Eligibility for Assistance

Regulations published in the *Federal Register* in August 2010 outlined the rules governing the definition of an *affirmative determination* of a community's eligibility for assistance.[7] Specifically, a community may apply for TAAC if on or after August 1, 2009 it met one or more of the following certifications:

1. a Department of Labor certification that a group of workers in the community are eligible to apply for Trade Adjustment Assistance for Workers (TAAW);
2. a Department of Commerce certification that a firm or firms located within the community are eligible for Trade Adjustment Assistance for Firms (TAAF); or
3. a Department of Agriculture certification that a group of agricultural producers in the community are eligible for Trade Adjustment Assistance to Farmers (TAA-Fm.).

In addition, EDA must determine that the community is or will be significantly affected by a threatened or expected or actual loss of jobs related to one of the certifications identified above. A community may submit an affirmative determination petition for designation as a community impacted by trade at least 180 days after the date of the most recent certification. The regulations also include a grandfather provision allowing communities that meet one of the three affirmative certifications related to workers, firms, or farmers issued between January 1, 2007, and August 1, 2009, to submit a petition for TAAC designation. The petition must be submitted before February 1, 2010.

The petition for an *affirmative determination* must be submitted to the appropriate EDA regional office and must include the following elements:

- sufficient information to allow EDA to make a determination that the petitioning community is significantly affected by the threat or actual loss of jobs associated with certification as a trade-impacted community; and
- information about the adverse impacts on the community from the actual or threatened loss of jobs.

The regulations direct EDA to use the petitioning community's most recent civilian labor force statistics when measuring such impacts. These data are available from the Department of Labor's Bureau of Labor Statistics.

Upon making an *affirmative determination* that a community qualifies for TAAC assistance, program regulations require EDA to promptly notify the state's governor and officials of the trade-impacted community of the availability of TAAC funds and other appropriated economic development assistance. The notification should also identify the means of obtaining TAAC and other federal economic development assistance, and the appropriate EDA regional office responsible for providing TAAC technical assistance to the community.

Provision of Technical Assistance

When EDA has determined that a community has been impacted by trade, program regulations direct EDA to provide comprehensive technical assistance to aid the community in developing or updating a strategic plan aimed at diversifying and strengthening the community's economy. In doing so, the community's strategic plan should identify trade-related impediments to economic developments and address economic adjustment and worker dislocation.

EDA is responsible for the coordination of federal assistance to trade impacted communities, including identifying all federal, state, and local resources available to address economic distress and assisting a trade-impacted community gain access to other federal programs. To facilitate this assistance

EDA is charged with establishing the Interagency Community Assistance Working Group (ICAWG) comprised of representatives from at least eight other federal agencies.[8] One of the principle roles of the ICAWG is to provide access to other federal programs when the trade-impacted community undertakes implementation grant activities.

Contents of the Strategic Plan

Program regulations require that a community must have an EDA-approved strategic plan before it can receive TAAC implementation grant funds. In developing its strategic plan each community is directed to seek the involvement of both public and private sector entities, including local educational institutions; federal, state, and local government entities serving the community; labor organizations representing workers in the impacted community; businesses; and local workforce investment boards.[9]

Program regulations outline elements that EDA must consider when evaluating a community's strategic plan. These elements can be grouped into three broad categories that are intended to assess a community's needs and assets, long-term economic adjustment prospects and commitments, and cost of implementation. Elements EDA will evaluate when reviewing a community's strategic plan are outlined in Table 1.

Implementation Grants

Implementation grants are awarded by EDA to fund projects and programs included in a community's approved strategic plan. An implementation grant may not exceed $5 million and may not cover more than 95% of the cost of a project or program. EDA must give priority in awarding grants to small and medium size communities. Program regulations also require EDA to submit an annual report to Congress identifying grants awarded during the fiscal year and assessing the impact of the grant activity on the affected community.

Program regulations identified six specific categories of eligible activities including

- infrastructure improvements, including site acquisition and preparation, construction, rehabilitation and equipping of a facility;
- market and industry research and analysis;
- technical assistance including feasibility studies, business networking and restructuring;
- public services;
- training; and

- other activities included in the strategic plan that satisfy statutory and regulatory requirements. [10]

Table 1. Elements EDA will Consider When Evaluating Strategic Plans.

Category	Elements
Community's Economic Adjustment Needs and Assets	• the economic development challenges and opportunities facing the community; • the community's capacity to achieve economic adjustment; • the strength and weakness of the community's economy; and • whether the education and training programs available to impacted area workers are consistent with the community's future employment needs.
Long-term Economic Adjustment Prospects and Commitments	• the role of community partners, including firms, education institutions, workforce investment boards, and labor organizations in developing and carrying out elements of the strategic plan; • description of projects to be undertaken; • how well the strategic plan will integrate with EDA's Comprehensive Economic Development Strategies (CEDS);[a] • description of the education and training programs available to workers in the impacted community and the future employment needs of the community; • how projects included in the strategic plan will facilitate economic adjustment; • articulation of the strategy for continuing economic adjustment after completion of projects funded by the strategic plan;
Cost elements	• projections of the cost of implementing the strategic plan • federal share of the cost of developing strategic plans may not exceed 75% .

Source: CRS, based on program regulations published in the Federal Register on 8/18/2009.

[a.] EDA also administers an economic adjustment assistance program targeted to distressed communities. Eligible communities must develop a CEDS as a requirement for assistance

Table 2. Authorization Levels for TAAC (in millions of dollars).

Fiscal Year		Authorization	
	Strategic Planning	Implementation Grants	Total
2009	25.000	125.000	150.000
2010	25.000	125.000	150.000
2011 1st Quarter	6.250	31.250	37.500

Source: P.L. 111-5.

Content of Implementation Grant Application

Implementation grant applications must include a copy of the EDA-approved strategic plan and a description of the proposed project or program to be funded. In addition, EDA will consider additional evaluation criteria identified in the applicable Federal Funding Opportunity announcement (FFO) when selecting recipients of implementation grants. Applicants seeking assistance under Subchapter B (community college and career training grants) or Subchapter C (sector partnership grants) must include in its implementation grant application a discussion of how projects or programs funded with implementation grants will use these two programs and other federal grant assistance.

Funding Authorizations and Appropriation Levels

The act authorized funding totaling $337.5 million for implementation and strategic planning grants for the period that includes FY2009, FY2010, and a 90 day period from October 1, 2010, to December 31, 2010 (see Table 2 of this report). For FY2009, Congress appropriated $40 million and directed that it be split between TAAC activities and Trade Adjustment Assistance for Firms (TAAF), which is also administered by the EDA. This was far less than the amount authorized. In addition, Congress did not provide instructions covering the distribution of funds between the two programs.

When it approved the Consolidated Appropriations Act of 2010, P.L. 111-117, Congress appropriated $15.8 million to be allocated between Trade Adjustment Assistance for Firms and Subchapter A (TAAC) activities.

TAAC Notice of Federal Funding Opportunity

On January 11, 2010, EDA published in the *Federal Register* a notice announcing the solicitation of applications for $37 million in TAAC planning and implementation grants and directed potential applicants to the grants.gov website. The notice of Federal Funding Opportunity established the criteria

EDA will used in ranking and awarding grants grant applications. EDA will use six weighted criteria in evaluating grant applications. They are:

- The extent to which the proposed activities support small and medium sized communities which are defined as communities with populations less than 100,000 persons (20%).
- The extent the proposed investment is targeted to the most severely trade impacted communities as measured by the number of persons receiving Trade Adjustment Assistance for workers (20%).
- The extent that the proposed activities will result in a high return on investment as measured by jobs created or retained, private and public sector funds leveraged and the use of best practices in the management of the project (20%).
- The extent the proposed activities will support regionalism, innovation, and entrepreneurship through the implementation of regional cluster strategies and the adaptation of technology for commercial usage (20%).
- The extent that the project supports global trade and competitiveness by supporting companies that have significant export potential (15%).
- The extent that the funded activity will promote the green economy through the use of renewable energy, energy efficiency and green building technology (5%).

The notice identified April 20, 2010, as the deadline for the submission of applications.[11]

Subchapter B—Community College and Career Training Grant (CC&CT)

Subchapter B directs the Department of Labor to award competitive grants to community colleges for use in developing or improving education and career training programs for persons eligible for Trade Adjustment Assistance for Workers (TAAW). The act limits the number and amount of grant funds an eligible institution may receive to not more than one grant of no more than $1 million.

Grant Requirements and Award Criteria

When applying for CC&CT grants applicants must include a description of:

- how funds will be used to develop or improve educational or career training programs available to eligible TAA workers;
- the extent to which eligible workers will benefit from the proposed program;
- how the project fits within the community's overall strategic plan;
- how the project relates to the Industry or Sector Partnership Grants;[12] and
- the institution's previous experience in providing education and training assistance to trade-impacted workers eligible for TAAW.

In addition, community colleges applying for assistance must demonstrate that they have undertaken outreach efforts involving prospective employers and other potential partners and collaborators in an attempt to identify deficiencies in existing education and career training opportunities. This outreach effort should also seek to:

- identify skills needed to take advantage of future opportunities;
- identify best practices undertaken by other institutions; and
- identify partnerships in the community that have sought or received Sector Partnership Grants.

Grant proposals must also include a discussion of how the proposed project will address the deficiencies identified in its outreach efforts and the extent to which employers have demonstrated a commitment to employing workers who would benefit from the proposed education or training activities.

Table 3. Authorization Levels for CC&CT (in millions of dollars).

Fiscal Year	Authorization
2009	40.000
2010	40.000
2011 1st Quarter	10.000

Source: P.L. 111-5.

Funds are awarded based on an evaluation of the likely employment opportunities to be made available to workers who complete the proposed educational or career training and whether existing educational and training programs lack the capacity to meet future demand.

Funding Authorization and Appropriations

The act authorizes funding totaling $90 million in grant assistance for the period covering FY2009, FY2010, and October 1, 2009, to December 31, 2010. The act prohibits grants from being used to meet the matching fund requirement of other federal grant programs; requires that funds be used to supplement but not supplant other federal, state and local funds; and requires Department of Labor to submit an annual report to Congress on the use and effectiveness of funded projects.

On March 30, 2010, the President signed the Health Care and Education Reconciliation Act of 2010, P.L. 111-152, which included $500 million for Subchapter B, CC&CT, grants for each of the fiscal years FY2011 through FY2014. The DOL has not yet published regulations governing the program or a notice of funding availability.

Subchapter C—Industry or Sector Partnership Grants

Subchapter C directs the Department of Labor to award Industry or Sector Partnership Grants (ISPG) to eligible public/private partnerships. Industry and sector partnerships are voluntary organizations located in communities eligible for trade adjustment assistance for workers, firms, or farmers. Such organizations must be comprised of representatives from industry associations; local, county, or state governments; businesses in the designated industry or sector, workforce investment boards; labor unions; and education institutions.

The act limits the number of grants an eligible industry partnership may be awarded by the Department of Labor to no more than one grant, or not more than $2.5 million, except in the case where the partnership is located in a community that does not receive Community College and Career Training grants. In such cases the amount may not exceed $3 million.

Grant Requirements and Award Criteria

Approved Industry and Sector Partnership Grant activities must be completed within three years. In general, grant proposals must:

- identify the industry or sector that will be the focus of the partnership;
- identify member organizations or entities involved in the partnership, including the lead agency;
- describe the goals and specific projects to be undertaken with grant funds;
- demonstrate that the partnership has the organizational capacity to carry out proposed projects; and
- explain whether the community has or will seek funding under the TAAC or community college and career training grant programs, or other federal programs, and how such assistance will be coordinated with industry and sector partnership grants.

Partnership Grants may be used to fund skill assessments and identify training and employment gaps. This includes using funds to:

- develop systems to better link skill workers with firms in the targeted industry;
- assist firms in obtaining access to qualified job applicants; and
- train new workers and retrain existing workers (including remedial skills training).

Funds may also be used to improve productivity, information and outreach activities, including the dissemination of information on best practices, the development of learning consortia comprised of small and medium size firms in an effort to lower the cost of training, and the identification of other resources including community college and career training grants.

DOL is directed to provide technical assistance to sector partnership entities to assist them in developing and administering sector partnership grants. In order to carry out this responsibility DOL may award technical assistance grants or contracts to one or more national or state organizations. It is also responsible for developing performance measures to be used by sector partnerships to measure progress in meeting goals outlined in their grant application. DOL is required to submit annual reports to Congress that include a listing of awards and an assessment of the program's impact.

Table 4. Authorization Levels for ISPG (in millions of dollars).

Fiscal Year	Authorization
2009	40.000
2010	40.000
2011 1st Quarter	10.000

Source: P.L. 111-5.

Funding Authorization and Appropriations

The TGAAA authorizes funding totaling $90 million in grant assistance for the period covering FY2009, FY2010, and October 1, 2009 through December 31, 2010. Grantees are prohibited from using grants to meet the matching fund requirement of other federal grant programs. The TGAAA expressly states that grant funds may supplement but not supplant other federal, state and local funds.

Congress did not include an appropriation for the program for FY2009 or FY2010. In addition, the Obama Administration did not request funding for the program for FY2011.

Subchapter D—General Provisions

Subchapter D includes a provision stating that a worker receiving trade adjustment assistance for workers (TAAW) will not be disqualified from or ineligible for assistance under any of the provisions of trade adjustment assistance to communities.

Issue Discussion

Appropriations

Congress appropriated significantly less funding than the $150 million it authorized for the TAAC program for FY2009. The Supplemental Appropriations Act of 2009, P.L. 111-32, included a $40 million appropriation to be used to fund both TAAC and the Trade Adjustment Assistance for Firms programs for FY2009.[13] In addition, the Consolidated appropriations Act for FY2010 included $15.8 million for TAAC and the Trade Adjustment

Assistance for Firms programs. In appropriating funds for communities and firms Congress did not include language in the supplemental act or the accompanying conference reports outlining how it intended the funds to be split between the two programs. Given the $5 million maximum amount that can be awarded for a single TAAC implementation grant, the combined $55.8 million appropriation will only fund a modest number of TAAC grant awards. In addition, grant funds must be used to fund strategic planning grant activities and trade adjustment assistance for firms.

Implementation Issues

Timeliness

EDA's implementation of the TAAC program may have been slowed by the process of filling vacant politically appointed positions. As a result, important agency decisions were delayed due to the absence of leadership. The agency's new Assistant Secretary for Economic Development, John R. Fernandez, was confirmed by the Senate on September 11, 2009. In addition, the appointment of a Director of Adjustment Assistance within EDA was also delayed. This absence of leadership may have also contributed to delay in the creation of the Interagency Community Assistance Working Group (ICAWG), charged with facilitating access to other federal programs in coordination with implementation grant activities under the TAAC program. EDA is the lead agency of the ICAWG.

Although EDA has published regulations governing Subchapter A, trade adjustment assistance to communities, the Department of Labor has not yet published regulations governing assistance to community colleges and sector partnership grants. The absence of such guidance may delay timely implementation of program activities and undermine the program's effectiveness. In addition, Congress did not immediately provide an initial appropriation for the Subchapter B (CC&CT) and Subchapter C (ISPG) grants for FY2009 or FY2010. Congress did appropriate $500 million for CC&CT grants for each of the fiscal years FY2011 through FY2014 when it passed the Health Care and Education Reconciliation Act of 2010, P.L. 111-152, which was signed by the President on March 30, 2010. This was well over a year after passing initial appropriations for Subchapter A activities. In addition, Congress has not yet appropriated funding for ISPG activities.

Interagency Coordination

The principal role of the ICAWG is to provide access to other federal programs when a TAAC designated community undertakes grant activities. The TAAC program's legislation and its rules encourage coordination with other economic development programs, directing EDA to identify possible grant assistance that might be available from other federal agencies, but does not guarantee trade adjustment assistance communities preference or priority in the awarding of such assistance.

In addition, in an effort to enhance effectiveness and avoid duplication, the law anticipates a high degree of coordination between EDA and the Department of Labor's Employment and Training Administration (ETA), which is responsible for the administration of the community college- based training program grants and sector partnership grants authorized under subchapters B and C of the act. For instance, the statute requires an educational institution submitting a grant proposal to ETA for CC&CT grant assistance to include a detailed description of the extent to which the proposed grant activity would fit within the strategic plan developed by a community eligible for TAAC assistance, and to explain how the CC&CT grant proposal relates to any project funded by a sector partnership grant. [14] In addition, the statute requires an entity seeking a sector or industry partnership grant to include in its grant application a discussion of whether the community impacted by trade has sought or received TAAC implementation grant funds, whether an eligible education institution had sought or received CC&CT grant funds, and how the eligible sector partnership entity will use grant assistance in coordination with TAAC, CC&CT, and funds from other grant sources.[15]

Targeting of Assistance

Congress may elect to amend the statue to more precisely define terms. For example, the legislation directs EDA to give priority to small and medium size communities when awarding implementation grants, but fails to establish or define what constitutes a small or medium size community. The definition of what constitutes a small or medium size community was not established in program regulations published in the *Federal Register*. This omission could lead to controversy if EDA does not target funds to appropriate sized communities consistent with congressional intent. EDA has since addressed this issue with the January 11, 2010, *Federal Register* publication of a notice soliciting applications for TAAC grants. The notice defined small and medium size communities as those whose population do not exceed 100,000 persons.

Duplication of Effort

Critics of the legislation may argue that the TAAC program duplicates the activities of other federal programs. This includes EDA's Economic Adjustment Assistance (EAA) program, which awards federal grant assistance to economically distressed communities regardless of the cause. EAA program assistance may be used to fund both the development of strategic plans (Comprehensive Economic Development Strategies—CEDS) and implementation grants intended to fund one or more the activities identified in the CEDS. Proponents may argue that trade adjustment assistance to communities is warranted because it is targeted to communities whose economic dislocation and distress can be traced to unfair trade competition.

Program Integration

The statute attempts to address an issue raised in previous reports and studies concerning the need to promote an integrated approach to addressing the impact of economic dislocation. A 2001 report by the General Accounting Office (GAO) found that

> Local officials believe that dislocated worker training programs are more effective and job placement much higher when strong links exist between training and local business needs.[16]

The TAAC grant program requires trade-impacted communities to seek the advice and involvement of a wide range of community partners when developing their strategic plans, including education institutions, labor organizations, firms, and workforce investment boards. These partners are not only essential in developing the strategic plan, but may also participate in its execution. For instance, the act also supports activities intended to identify and address deficiencies in existing education and career training opportunities available to eligible TAA workers through the use of community colleges. It also encourages the creation of public-private partnerships focusing on skills and employment assessments, and training activities by funding sector partnership grants. Both grant programs (CC&CT and Sector Partnerships) require that the recipient of funds identify the link between the proposed grant and the community's strategic plan developed with TAAC funding.

End Notes

[1] U.S. Department of Commerce, Economic Development Administration, "Solicitation of Applications for the Community Trade Adjustment Assistance Program," 75 *Federal Register* 1345, January 11, 2011. Concurrently, EDA published the application at the following Grants.gov website: http://www.grants announce.do;jsessionid=XvrGL12QpLbpQBvvh7yMT8w1 1G1XMc2LW9LFkNXhbVKz4GhY9jvD !-2823 1359.

[2] Business Cycle Dating Committee, *Determination of the December 2007 Peak in Economic Activity*, National Bureau of Economic Research, Cambridge, MA, December 2008, http://wwwdev.nber.org/cycles

[3] P.L. 111-5, Division B, Title I, Subtitle I; 123 Stat. 367.

[4] P.L. 93-618; 19 U.S.C. 1978.

[5] For a discussion of trade adjustment assistance programs to firms, farmers, and workers see the following CRS reports: CRS Report RS20210, *Trade Adjustment Assistance for Firms: Economic, Program, and Policy Issues*, by J. F. Hornbeck; CRS Report R40206, *Trade Adjustment Assistance for Farmers*, by Remy Jurenas; CRS Report RL34383, *Trade Adjustment Assistance (TAA) for Workers: Current Issues and Legislation*, by John J. Topoleski, and Trade Adjustment Assistance (TAA) for Workers: Current Issues and Legislation, by John J. Topoleski.

[6] P.L. 111-5, Division B, Title I, Subtitle I, Part III; 123 U.S.C. 401. The Trade Act of 1974, P.L. 93-618 (19 U.S.C. 2371, 88 Stat. 2035) as originally enacted included provisions authorizing trade adjustment assistance for communities. The original act also included a provision (Sec. 284 of P.L. 93-618), 88 Stat. 2041) terminating the program on September 30, 1982.

[7] Department of Commerce, Economic Development Administration, "Revisions to the Trade Adjustment Assistance for Firms Program Regulations and Implementation Regulations for the Community Trade Adjustment Assistance Program," 74 *Federal Register* 41592 - 41603, August 18, 2009.

[8] ICAWG includes representatives from the Department of Agriculture, Department of Defense, Department of Education, Department of Labor, Department of Housing and Urban Development, Department of Health and Human Services, Department of Transportation, and Small Business Administration.

[9] Created by the Workforce Investment Act of 1998, workforce investment boards are substate regional entities charged with directing federal, state, and local workforce development resources. See 112 Stat. 954.

[10] Department of Commerce, Economic Development Administration, "Implementation Grants for Impacted Communities," 74 *Federal Register* 41597, August 18, 2009.

[11] A synopsis of grant requirements and links to the grant announcement and grant applications for the TAAC Federal Funding Opportunity can be accessed at http://www07.grants search. do;j sessionid=qqR3LDvPlb64ztX2WGWncxsdF25DLLnnv2v2Df4Jn1XfshNwkMpw!3642889 8?oppId=5 1071 &mode=VIEW.

[12] Industry or Sector Partnership Grants were also authorized with the passage of TGAAA of 2009. Funds are to be awarded competitively by the Department of Labor and are intended to encourage the development of public private partnerships focusing on the development of a skilled workforce.

[13] 123 Stat. 1860.

[14] 19 U.S.C. 278(c)(4)(A)(iii) and (iv) at 123 Stat. 407.

[15] 19 U.S. C. 279A(e)(F) at 123 Stat. 411.

[16] U.S. General Accounting Office (now known as the Government Accountability Office), *Trade Adjustment Assistance Experiences of Six Trade-Impacted Communities*, GAO-01-838, August 2001, p. 4, http://www.gao.gov/ new.items/d01 838.pdf.

CHAPTER SOURCES

The following chapters have been previously published:

Chapter 1 – This is an edited reformatted and augmented version of a Congressional Research Service publication, report RS20210, dated February 14, 2011.

Chapter 2 – This is an edited reformatted and augmented version of a Congressional Research Service publication, report R40206, dated February 14, 2011.

Chapter 3 – This is an edited reformatted and augmented version of a Congressional Research Service publication, report RS22718, dated January 7, 2011.

Chapter 4 – This is an edited reformatted and augmented version of a Congressional Research Service publication report RS22761 dated January 30, 2008.

Chapter 5 – This is an edited reformatted and augmented version of a United States Government Accountability Office publication, report GAO-07-994T, dated June 14, 2007.

Chapter 6 – This is an edited reformatted and augmented version of a Congressional Research Service publication, report R40863, dated April 9, 2010.

INDEX

A

B

C

D

E